Human
Relations

COMPLETE MANAGEMENT LIBRARY

Volume XII

Lowell S. Trowbridge *Associate Professor of Human Relations, College of Business Administration, Boston University*

HUMAN
RELATIONS

National Foremen's Institute
Bureau of Business Practice
National Sales Development Institute
WATERFORD, CONNECTICUT

COMPLETE MANAGEMENT LIBRARY
VOLUME XII

© MCMLXIII Prentice-Hall, Inc.
Waterford, Connecticut

LIBRARY OF CONGRESS CATALOG CARD NO. 63-8563

PRINTED IN THE UNITED STATES OF AMERICA

Fourth Printing, August, 1968

PREFACE

Because man has evolved through social groups, we are in constant relationships with other people. This book concerns such relationships called "human relations," primarily as they occur in our present economic culture and particularly in business and industry.

Some of the material in this book may be defined as nothing more than "organized common sense." On the other hand, a few new ideas may require the reader to ponder a few moments on whether they fit into his ways of thinking and living. It is hoped that these ideas will be worth pondering, and improve the way in which some people relate with each other.

The writer, and others in the field of human relations (also called "behavioral science") believe that man has the capacity for greater understanding and cooperation than he has accomplished thus far. Those who work with human relations realize that the principles described in this handbook have actually changed their lives and made them happier and more effective individuals. They have also influenced the lives of some people with whom they come in contact.

The Plan of This Book

Each chapter begins with a "case" describing a situation. It is hoped that the reader will read these carefully, then close the book and think about the situation for a few minutes. We hope that he will look objectively and critically to see where he approves and where he disapproves. This will enable him to check his thinking as he reads the remaining part of the chapter. The end of each chapter has a critical evaluation of the original situation.

Thus the reader may compare his reactions to ours and the way in which we have attempted to apply the ideas in the chapter to a particular situation. It is hoped that the reader will then begin to look for other situations in his daily life where he can apply the principles.

This book and its ideas have been made possible because people are individuals, and each makes his contributions, constructively or destructively, to the society around him.

Effective human relations offers a great reward to the leader in business or industry. By dealing knowledgeably with other human beings, he rewards himself while helping them to greater satisfactions and achievements.

TABLE OF
CONTENTS

vii

TABLE OF CONTENTS

CHAPTER ONE

What Is
Human Relations?

In the early 1900's, industry was trying to increase productivity by utilizing engineering approaches. By the 1920's, the language of industry was full of allusions to "straight line production", "spaced rest periods," "the right man for the job," and "the one best way to do a job." This was the language of the "efficiency expert," concerning the application of principles of scientific management attributed to Frederick Taylor. Human beings (workers) were seen as production units of certain capacities under ideal conditions. It was believed that if the worker could be taught certain sequences of movement, pre-placement of work materials and tools, and was placed in a correct physical setting, his productivity would increase. Frank Gilbreth (portrayed in the film *Cheaper by the Dozen*) espoused time-and-motion studies. Hugo Munsterberg, psychologist on the faculty of Harvard University, studied Boston Elevated Railroad operators with high accident rates, and dis-

1

covered the influence of color blindness and other physical defects. By 1920, applied psychology had advanced to such a point that industry began to avail itself of the new methods for selecting and training employees, and improving industrial working conditions. However, despite the vast literature which had accumulated by the 1930's no attention had been paid to the fact that all workers had social relationships with other human beings, which might affect their productivity. The *human being* had been completely neglected while the human *machine* received all the attention.

In the 1920's, an industrial experiment in working conditions at a Western Electric plant had an enormous impact upon industry many years later. This is the famous Hawthorne Plant experiment, of which the reader has probably heard. The experiment was devised to study a small group of women workers who assembled electrical relays. The women were isolated in a room where their physical working conditions were altered from time to time, while their job productivity was carefully recorded. By the time the Depression made it advisable to discontinue the experiment, some astonishing results had been accumulated. The women's productivity went up, even when, at the end of the experiment, working conditions returned to what they had been years before. This outcome was baffling. Years passed before the reasons for it were known. Interviews with employees eventually revealed that *the* most important thing about the job is *not* the heat, light, humidity, tool placement, salary, etc. (although each is important). Crucial were the social relationships among workers, and between workers and supervisors or higher management. The high rise in productivity among the women at Hawthorne was due to the special social freedom and warmth they enjoyed during the experiment. Repetitions of the Hawthorne experiment have borne this out.

At approximately the same time (late 1920's to early 1930's), the R. H. Macy department store in New York City set another precedent. Macy's viewpoint was that the individual worker has certain problems, not only in his job relationships, but also with his family and friends. The store was probably the first large business firm to have a psychiatric consultant on its staff. He brought to the company the new knowledge about the emotional life of human beings which Freud and others had contributed.[1]

The new idea that the worker was a person with feelings and emotions rather than just a production machine was expanded in the late 1930's and the early 1940's by world tension. During World War II, industry was hard-pressed to maintain necessary war production. Experiments were made in leadership and personnel counseling. Studies were conducted on race and social relations. Wartime required additional management services to workers. Personnel functions often included finding homes for workers, providing transportation, making recreation possible. It was seen that the fatigued worker was an inefficient worker. Business and industry took the "giant step" of recognizing the worker as a person whose emotional needs required attention. Baseball and bowling, public swimming pools, and com-

[1] Reference to the work at Macy's is to be found in *Human Nature at Work*, by Jean L. Shepard, Harper & Bros., 1938.

munity problems began to engage the attention of industry. The worker's community relationships were seen to intimately affect his work efficiency.

The Advent of "Human Relations"

Realizing the need of management for understanding people and their relationships, schools and colleges of business, as well as sociology departments in liberal arts colleges, began to turn their attention to the organizing of material and the development of teaching methods for the training of their students in this general area. The knowledge from the research in the fields of the social sciences—anthropology, sociology, cultural anthropology, applied psychology, social psychology, etc. —were brought together. From this accumulation of data came principles and theories that could be applied to everyday living. In other words, knowledge from social sciences was to be used in developing understanding of human individuals and their relationships with each other, as they occur in the daily living in the home, community, family and job.

This book considers, primarily, understanding and use of these principles as they apply in the working world. As material is presented, there will be occasions when applications in related fields will be mentioned, because we cannot isolate an individual's working life from the other influences which affect his working situation.

CHAPTER TWO

Organizational Structure and Human Relations

Setting: the personnel department. Speaking: the personnel manager. "I've got the dirty end of the stick again! Area B foreman is afraid to tell his man that he's through. They hired the guy against our advice, they gave him two more chances—again, against our advice —and now they have the infernal gall to want *me* to do their firing! That's their job—they hired him—let *them* fire him! Firing isn't a staff function—these line men are shirkers!"

This commonplace situation represents some of the more vexing aspects of organization. Any organization is concerned with human relations. The very word *organization* implies that people are relating with one another for a certain purpose. In the work world we are, of course, very conscious of organization. The first step in establishing any new enterprise is to set up a "table of organization". The first requirement in analyzing a "sickness" in any existing business or industry is to study the table of organization, in order to understand the inter-relationships of people, and the chain of command.

Yet, a table of organization can be and often is a rather sterile picture of the total enterprise. It may show how people *should* inter-relate, but the actual contacts, communication, orders and complaints may go far afield of the designated pathways shown on the chart. Consequently, recent years have seen a great deal of study on how to present organizations in a more dynamic and realistic way.

The Formal Organization

In setting up a table of organization, it is customary to know the company's goals and structure the organization in terms of accomplishing them. The company's goal always involves a product—either goods or services. Two kinds of employee functions must be considered: Production of the goods and services, and maintenance of the organization itself. The production of goods or services is usually considered a "line" function; maintenance of the organization, a "staff" responsibility.

6

PYRAMID CHARTS

When these two functions—production and maintenance—are charted, a triangular design often emerges. (The usual shape is the pyramid.) At the top are the stockholders, the board of directors, and the president, or chairman or manager. Vertical or slanting lines radiate from the position of chairman, and indicate areas of responsibility (and authority) for phases of production. These are positions of "line" members.

Horizontal lines usually represent areas or departments of maintenance, referred to as "staff." Typical staff functions are personnel, finance, and public relations. The pyramidal form of the typical table of organization derives historically from military antecedents. It emphasizes authority and control rather than the actual functions of organization members. It cannot possibly include the position of every employee. It implies that people higher in the organization (closer to the chairman) have authority over people who are lower. Staff people ordinarily have authority only over their own departmental employees. Elsewhere, staff functions in an advisory capacity. There are, of course, exceptions. The pyramidal design may be very flat, with one individual "in charge of" many workers. On the other hand, it may be very high, indicating that supervisory contact and control is almost immediate. In either event, an individual's place in the chart comes to have great meaning for him. In business and industry, "who you are" means less than "what you are" on the organization chart. We all recognize the implications of the

7

phrase "low man on the totem pole." (More will be said of this when we discuss status later in this chapter.)

THE "CIRCLE" CHART

Attempts have been made to depict organizational structure in designs other than the traditional pyramid. One proposed method charts organization as a series of concentric circles. The core or nucleus represents "boss" (president, general manager, managing director, or some similar position). The next circle represents managers of departments or major areas; the position of each relates to neighboring departments on the same level with which there are especially close relationships. Subordinates represent the third circle, their subordinates a fourth circle, and so on. This circular representation tries to reduce the "totem pole" idea by de-emphasizing authority pathways. Such charts are mere euphemisms which try to hide or "tone down" the harsh realities of the line-staff hierarchy.

FLAWS IN THE PYRAMID

The conventional pyramidal line/staff organizational plan has several inherent weaknesses which produce perplexing human relations problems. A major weakness is that positions toward the top of the pyramid, be it "flat" or "high," require greater diversity of technical knowledge *plus* policy-making ability *plus* human relations skill. An outstanding example of this is in the structure of the U.S. Federal Government, where supreme authority resides in the presidency. The Presidency of the country (top of line authority) is supplemented by Cabinet members and presidential "advisers" who operate in a consulting capacity (equivalent to staff in business and industry). Thus, the managing director of a large corporation or the president of the United States is a single man who is expected to be "all things to all people." Since he will be less than perfect, he will make errors. His errors will be costly in money and in human feelings.

A second problem of the pyramidal line/staff structure is communication. Today, many of the technical problems of communication, such as volume of sale in a particular area, cost per item of production, inventory, and similar data, are being solved by the various electronic information-sorting devices in organizations that can afford them. But the problem of communication from one person to a subordinate or a superior remains with us. How much *can* you explain? How much *will* you explain when your communication may give offense? What about communication from line to staff and vice-versa? A recent trend has been to meet such problems by altering the organizational structure into committees.

Committee Organization

This resembles straight-line, and line/staff organization, except that a group of individuals, rather than a single individual, represents a position of authority. The thought is "two heads are better than one." The intelligence, training and skills of several people are used to make a composite of the executive or managerial personality. The assumption that more participants provide more and better solutions to problems seems to be valid, judging by the wealth of laudatory literature on the subject during the past 10 years. However, committee organization has a huge drawback—it is extremely time-consuming. You have undoubtedly attended non-business committee meetings, such as the discussion in a town meeting of where to put the local incinerator. If so, you may have been tempted to discard the democratic method of free discussion and group decision-making in favor of the old-fashioned, military, dictator-type, time-saving immediate decision! Business and industry have this same problem. They often reject the benefits of committee organization, because they can't afford the time involved.

Another version of committee organization is known as consultive-management in business and industry, because the function of the committees is to *advise*. The committees contain either staff internal to the organization, or expert consultants from outside the organization. They render reports and advise. Line officials then make the decisions. Although consultive management will probably grow in the future, the conservatism of United States business and industry suggests that most of us will have to wrestle with the problems of the line/staff pyramidal organization for our own lifetimes.

Status and Role

The table of organization, as usually conceived, in no way indicates the status of the various people on it, although we usually concede that the higher on it a person is, the more prestige he has and the greater his status. In other words, the "big bosses" are at the top. However, it is obvious that many staff positions have considerable prestige. Certainly, the engineering departments of companies today consider themselves to have a lot.

In regard to role, the table of organization rarely explains exactly what the duties of each position are. This is unfortunate. Everybody in the table of organization has some sort of direct or indirect relationship with everybody else in it.

From the human relations point of view, all these individuals must work together in order to produce goods or services for which the organization has been set up.

One unfortunate thing about the usual table of organization is that the people "at the top" are usually thought of as the prestige people. As has been mentioned, some companies' tables of organization show the people in authority at the center. The rest of the organization is represented in circles about the center, in the way in which ripples of water move out from the point where force is exerted. This puts the laboring force on the outside edges of the organization, but not at the bottom.

This may make people feel they have more prestige

11

and that their role in the organization has some importance in the whole dynamic concept. It also is possible that adults on the outside "see through" this well-intentioned device, in the same way a first-grader returns from a school reporting, "I'm a robin-reader, they're the good ones—Mickie is an oriole—that's the dummy group."

Control

The management function in any organization has three aspects of control. The basic one is "accountability." Accountability does not permit "passing the buck," but stays with the individual to whom it belongs. *He* alone is accountable, and must explain why he, or his subordinates, did not perform according to organizational standards. A second aspect of control is responsibility. Responsibility is often a delegation or entrustment of a task from the accountable individual to another who will "see that it gets done." The third aspect of control is authority. The person with authority gives the actual orders.

Sometimes an individual is accountable, responsible and authoritative at the same time.

Most of the time, however, the executive will delegate responsibility and authority, often in unequal shares. Think of the dilemma of an "acting-manager in charge of—" who is assigned the responsibilities of the absent manager but has not been given the authority to act. This is like telling the baby-sitter "You're in charge but don't spank or boss the children." In the delegation of managerial duties, we must tell or be told *what* is delegated. If the situation is not structured and specified, the delegate's hands are tied. He will not act efficiently, he will be scolded or punished, and he will experience keen resentment and frustration.

Many people in prestige situations want maximum authority to remain in their hands. They feel that all decision-making should be within the upper organizational strata. This was the idea of the great entrepreneurs such as Carnegie, Ford, and DuPont. The day of the great dictatorships seems to be passing in business and industry as well as in military life. Yet the remnants of extreme authoritarianism still plague us. One mark of the competent executive is the ability to delegate responsibility and authority to suitable personnel. Unwillingness to do so suggests great vulnerability and insecurity on his part.

Sometimes, decisions of a trivial nature must be made in "high" places because of communication difficulties, through ignorance, lack of courage, or fear of reprisals. "It's no skin . . . ." is a common vulgarism indicating unwillingness to accept responsibilities which can be passed on higher. The problem of delegation of responsibility and authority leads directly into the difficulties related to span of control.

SPAN OF CONTROL

As we indicated in the foregoing, the more the individual shirks responsibility, (or his superior refuses to delegate responsibility or authority) the longer the postponement of the decision-making process. The executive who jealously retains every fragment of authority possible is confronted with the need to make numerous decisions. This is time-consuming—for him and for those whose future activities depend upon his decisions or orders.

It has been often written that one man's direct span of authority should comprise no more than six persons. This rule is more honored in the breach than the observance. Where work is highly specialized and common to all members of a department, the supervisory span might well be 100 or more individuals without forfeiting efficiency. However, where work is diversified and involves individual responsibilities, the authority span may need to be much smaller. Theoretical formulations like the "rule of six" are not always practical. There is no simple formula. A "trouble-spot" is often the span of authority. An example is the common utilization under "personnel" of obligations towards payroll, attendance, safety, applicant-screening, appraisal interviewing, and other "staff" responsibilities. A span of authority which embraces all these functions is too much for one individual to supervise in any but a very small organization.

Overlapping Authority.   Related to span of control is the subordinate's complaint of "too many bosses." In the old days of strictly "straight-line" organization, each worker was responsible to a single boss. When organization evolved into a functional combination of line and staff, greater flexibility resulted. This greater flexibility had a price however. "Everyone got into the act." Thus, today, a production worker is responsible to his foreman. But he may also receive a reprimand from a staff official in charge of safety for improper conditions about his machine. His union may demand that he refuse to do some work not in his job description, although his foreman has requested it.

Another commonplace example is the stenographic pool supervisor who is responsible for a particular kind and quantity of output during certain prescribed hours, and under certain prescribed schedules of priority. Demands are made upon the stenographic service by some "high" executive—demands which do not conform to these regulations but which are qualified as "emergency." We all recognize the frustrations of the individual with too many bosses.

From the point of view of good human relations, it is obviously extremely frustrating to have duties and responsibilities while lacking the necessary authority. It is also annoying when every decision an individual proposes must be approved by someone "up above" in the table of organization. Subordinates need opportunities for responsibility, to help them to learn. The good administrator offers his workers abundant opportunity to exercise and improve their abilities, and to be promoted to more responsible positions. The executive who denies them such opportunities reveals his own fears and insecurities. He also denies his subordinates deserved opportunities for their own growth and development.

It has been said that "no department should be greater than what one manager can control." This means that an executive should know something about every one of the people for whom he is responsible. This indicates the appropriate size of the span of control. The manager must "keep in touch" and give recognition to each subordinate. He entrusts routine decisions to those below him, leaving himself free for the greater problems of developing his department or plant efficiency, and furthering the growth of his subordinates. When a subordinate makes an error of judgment, his errors are explained, not punished. If the errors he can make are enormously expensive, in dollars or good will, then he should not be entrusted with decision-making of such magnitude until he has proved himself with lesser problems.

Power

When an individual joins an organization, the table of organization defines his power only in respect to his authority. His position is shown, along with the positions of people "above or over" him and those "under" him. This is seldom an accurate way of appraising his power. Although the President of the United States is Commander-in-chief of the Army, the recruit is probably far more in awe of his sergeant.

PRESTIGE

A source of power not revealed by the organization chart is prestige, or the reputation that a particular person or position has as a source of power. Prestige often depends upon the historical development of the company, and possibly upon the community in which it functions. A position may hold prestige in one company, and none in another. Prestige is often developed through tradition. Thus, a newcomer to an organization may be surprised to find that although he has authority, responsibility, and high earnings, his position may lack prestige. One example is the observation that the secretary to the general plant manager usually enjoys greater prestige than the secretary to the purchasing agent, although the salaries of both may be the same and the purchasing agent's secretary may actually be in a position of being able to save the company a great deal of money. Certain positions automatically carry a considerable amount of prestige and give the incumbent unusual power and influence.

THE PERIPHERAL WORKER

Another quite unofficial source of power which contradicts the organization chart is that of the worker whose position is entirely peripheral on the chart. One member of a production line who slows down can reduce the output of all. In maintenance, failure to repair a break-down promptly can also reduce production. At an important ceremony of a large organization, where internationally-famous dignitaries were present, there was an uncomfortable delay while the janitor had to be found to unlock the room which held the ceremonial properties. Although his oversight was not deliberate, his power was obvious. Labor disputes often reveal unsuspected sources of power. A strike of payroll clerks can close down a national transportation system.

Related to prestige is status, or rank. This is often symbolically expressed as an important aspect of personal attainment. Persons sensitive to and interested in human relations do well to be aware of such symbols. It is a well-publicized fact that executive status is shown in some organizations by the office furnishings. A bare floor means lower status than one with a rug. The office with wall-to-wall carpeting belongs to a more important executive. He in turn, aspires to an office with an oriental rug or a plant box. It is also widely recognized that the junior executive does well to think it over before he buys a car of the same model and year as that of his superior.

Line Versus Staff

One source of friction within an organization is when the staff people "interfere with" the people in the line. The role of staff people in relation to the line people has been subject to a considerable amount of comment and writing. Usually, the table of organization does not clearly indicate how much responsibility and authority staff people have in regard to people in the line. The personnel department is usually a staff function, but has a great deal of responsibility in regard to "the line."

An example is the question of whether or not an employee was dishonest. The staff personnel man was asked to interview the employee and advise respecting termination. He refused to do this until he was given the authority to say whether the employee would be fired or would continue in his position, depending on what the interview elicited.

There is no cut-and-dried answer in regard to the matter of the relationship between staff and line. General policies, rather than strict rules and regulations, are needed. It is sometimes difficult to indicate such policy relationships in a table of organization. If this difficulty exists, a written statement of policy can be made and reaffirmed by various means.

In a recent situation requiring some redesigning of machinery, the designer was referred to the engineering department. This, of course, was a staff function. There was concern over the problem of the outcome of any designing the engineers did. In order to solve the situation, two engineers were assigned to work in the department with the regular line employees, in order to gain first-hand knowledge of what had to be done. A committee was then formed, including the head of the engineering department, the head of the purchasing department, and the head of the production department. This committee had the authority to make the final decisions as to what would be done after the recommendation of the two engineers had been received.

The Team Approach

With the growth of human relations has come the awareness that a small group, working as a team, can often come up with sounder ideas than can a single individual. This is due in part to "more heads being better than one," and also to the fact that members of the team may come from different but related backgrounds. Therefore, each member of the team may see an aspect of the problem which others ignore. The team approach has worked particularly well in problems of medical care, where the team (internist, surgeon, nurse, social worker, etc.) integrates contributions towards the total care of the patient. It also works extremely well when the members of the "committee" or "team" have experienced group dynamics training which was human relations-oriented. (The training and use of small groups will be discussed later.)

Likert[1] writes: "American management will make full use of the potential capacity of its human resources only when each person in an organization is a member of one or more well knit, effectively functioning work groups that have high skills of interaction and a high performance goal. If every organization was made up of cohesive, effectively functioning teams, we could predict great increased productivity and substantially greater human satisfaction than now exists.

"Consequently, management should deliberately endeavor to build these teams, linking them into an overall organization by means of people who hold over-lapping group memberships. The superior in the bottom group is a subordinate to the next group and so on up through the organization. Staff as well as line processes should be characterized by the team part or function. Throughout the pattern of organization, the supervisory processes used should develop and strengthen team spirit and group functioning."

It seems obvious that if one is to understand the human relations factors within an organization, he must first look at the total organization. He must realize that

[1] Likert, Rensis, *Developing Patterns in Management,* pamphlet of American Management Association, General Management Series, Number 182, 1956.

much of the dynamics of organization is not adequately represented in a table of organization. In fact, such a chart may be most misleading. He must then go beyond the formal picture, to informal organization.

The Informal Organization

People build relationships with one another when they associate either at work or in their family and community life. People with common interests tend to band together. Such combinations may comprise people of the same religion, national background, family ties, or whose personality needs can be mutually met in an informal relationship.

The informal relationship within an organization does exist, and must be accepted and understood. Informal organizations have their means of communication and their leaders as do formal organizations. The formal leader will be discussed in the chapter on "leadership." At the moment, we will consider the role and function of the informal organization.

Basically, informal organizations serve individual needs. Some of these informal structures may be extremely strong and may exert considerable influence. Older employees who have built an informal structure may make it very difficult for new employees to "break into" the "in group." Although the new employees are doing perfectly satisfactory work and developing loyalty to the company, they may feel excluded, and therefore be unhappy in their work relationships.

A sensitive supervisor is aware of the informal structure and comes to an understanding of what it means. Loyalty within an informal group can often be used to get people to work beyond formal expectations, because of their pride in working together and seeing a job well done. Another very important aspect of the informal organization is the matter of communications. The speed and the direction of a rumor circulated through an organization will tell a great deal about informal structure. A rumor may start in Department A, and suddenly turn up in Department K a few hours later, yet there are no apparent lines of communication. Investigation may show that a member of Department K once worked in Department A, and has informal associations there. Individuals happen to meet in the cafeteria for coffee. The more closely knit a group is, the faster rumor moves. Its pathway shows informal relationships.

The wise manager knows this, and uses the informal organization to great advantage. We will come back to this in the chapter on communications.

Summary

The situation at the beginning of the chapter represents a typical organizational error. Staff and line responsibilities regarding firing have not been adequately thought out and *defined*.

CHAPTER THREE

Morale

Case Study in Poor Morale

Jack Curtis, vice-president in charge of manufacturing and personnel of the Cestus Manufacturing Company, called Fred Loring, his personnel manager, into his office one day.

"Fred," he said, "I attended a meeting last night and there was a lot of talk about periodic employee evaluations and stuff like that. I guess we don't do anything like that, do we?"

"No, Jack, we don't," Fred replied. "Production seems to be OK, and we don't have too much of a labor turnover, so we let well enough alone."

"Yeah, maybe you're right. If we start asking questions, maybe we'll stir up a hornet's nest. Let's let sleeping dogs lie."

Two weeks later, the vice-president called Fred in again.

"For God's sake, Fred, what's happened? I understand Ed Cole, the finishing room supervisor, has walked out, and already eight other men have quit, and more

23

may be going. Production seems shot to hell. What's going on, anyway?"

"Gee, Jack, I don't know. Everything seemed OK like it always is, until we posted the vacation schedule. Ed Cole came in, ranting and raving, and seemed upset mostly because we hadn't consulted him about the schedule. I guess some of the boys were sore about it, too, but you couldn't talk to them. I can't see why they're so burned up. The schedule is about the same as last year and the year before, so we didn't bother talking to anyone about it. Two years ago, when we made up that schedule, we did talk to Ed and got his ideas, and we've just gone along on that basis."

This is obviously a problem of poor morale among some of the men. Business and industrial morale is usually defined as a positive attitude towards the work environment and towards voluntary exertion and cooperation in the best interests of the organization being served. Low morale is characterized by its symptoms —strikes, grievances, slowdowns, absenteeism, low productivity, etc. Plant morale, like individual health, requires constant vigilance and preventative care lest deterioration and ill health set in. Either an individual or a group can have high or low morale.

Productivity and Morale

It is generally thought that there is a close relationship between productivity and morale. Let us examine the evidence for this widespread belief, before considering morale. There are many measures of productivity.

Volume of production maintained or increased is one. Another is the ratio of cost to production. Still another is the flow of current production in relation to "back orders," "future orders" and the maintenance of a reasonable inventory. Productivity is usually evaluated both quantitatively and qualitatively, according to a variety of standard methods.

The appraisal of morale is quite different, and extremely difficult. The first difficulty is the ambiguity of the term itself. The zest for work may be appraised by questionnaires, interviews, and other methods, and found to bear little or no relation to productivity. Chris Argyris[1] writes of a situation in which morale was found to be low, (if morale is equated with enthusiasm, zest, or energy) yet the pay scale was sufficiently high so that workers were willing to work and produce. In fact, they did produce satisfactorily, despite their low morale.

Another lack of clarity in definition of morale is found in situations where worker morale is high in relation to the union but low in respect to management. If morale is equated with productivity, we have the situation dramatized in the beginning of this chapter, where managers are "sitting on top of a volcano"—with unsuspected poor morale "about to blow the lid off." Still another paradox is present in situations where morale is high, and everyone is "happy as a clam," but the work doesn't get out! These three contradictory types of situations emphasize the problem of accurately measuring a condition which we cannot clearly define.

[1] Argyris, Chris, *Personality and Organization,* Harper & Bros., 1957.

What Is Morale?

The term which predates morale is "esprit de corps," meaning group spirit. To understand it, we must know to what group it refers. Group loyalty differs from one situation to another. In education, for example, we have the loyalty of students to each other. As the attendance slip is passed about, a student may sign not only his own name but the name of an absent friend in carefully disguised handwriting. In industry, we can have high group loyalty within a production group, so that slackening by one of its members will be concealed from the foreman. At the same time, we can have disloyalty towards management and the revelation of company secrets, subtle sabotage, slow-downs, and other aggressive acts.

Thomas J. Luck[2] writes, in his book *Personnel Audit and Appraisal,* "Morale is a by-product of a social equilibrium or organization in which individuals and groups working together can find such human satisfactions as will make them identify their personal desires temporarily with those of the group or organization." He goes on to expand this idea by writing . . . "morale should be defined as that attitude of an individual which may be conditioned by groups within which he participates and enables him to identify the achievement of his personal objectives with the organization's objectives. That is, the individual feels that he can best fulfill

[2] Luck, Thomas J., *Personnel Audit and Appraisal,* McGraw-Hill Book Co., 1955.

his desires by working to achieve the objectives of his company."

ATTITUDES

The quotations just given reflect the trend in business and industry to discard the comprehensive and vague term *morale*, and substitute for it *plural attitudes of the individual as related to his work*. Attitudes are "mental sets" or habits. They represent a readiness of an individual to respond to situations on the basis of his past learning. He no longer has to reflect and choose among alternatives of behavior, he is "ready, set, on the mark . . ." You yourself have attitudes towards each of the following. Read them and see!

Management   Unions   Yankees   Income Tax Return
Southerners   Italians   Politicians

Your reaction to some of the words on the foregoing list was personal, and often emotional. You may have forgotten the origin of the feelings you experienced, or possibly may never have known the reason for them. Yet, toward some of these words your attitude was positive, warm, enthusiastic. Toward others, you felt hostility, disapproval, resistance. Perhaps others were neutral for you and evoked no "for or against" feelings at all.

Workers develop attitudes toward "the company," "management," "unions," "safety rules," "appraisal interviews," "department conferences" and other aspects of intra-organizational life. When an occurrence re-affirms an individual's attitude, he rejoices and strengthens it. If an experience contradicts an attitude, the individual is disturbed and defensive. If there are many such experiences, his attitude may weaken or alter in the other direction.

Management today concerns itself very much with the formation of "good" attitudes and the amendment of attitudes unfavorable to the advancement of the organization's goals. An illustration of this is the literature on "image." The U.S. government is trying to improve the "image" of the United States held by other nationals. Large industries and businesses are at work forming or modifying their "corporate images." The presentation of "the image" is an attempt to build up favorable attitudes. An important part of the human relations program of many companies is to determine the attitudes of workers, anticipate their behavior, and modify their attitudes where this seems desirable. In this chapter we shall continue to concern ourselves with the recognition of morale or attitudes and in a later chapter shall indicate how human relations training can re-mold such attitudes.

Among the worker attitudes which have been explored and which seem to be important factors in what we call morale are the following:

1. How adequate does the individual feel is his immediate supervision? The immediate supervisor is the worker's point of contact with the organization.
2. How satisfying does the individual find his job? Most people like a job which uses at least some of their skills, and where they can give a good account of themselves.
3. Are relationships with fellow employees reasonably

satisfying? Almost all human beings have a strong need for acceptance by others.

4. Can the individual feel himself part of a worthwhile structure (the organization) with a worthwhile goal?
5. Does the individual feel adequately rewarded, by pay and by recognition, when he compares himself with those within and without the organization?
6. Does the worker feel self-confident and effective in his personal, home, and community relationships? Special worries or problems with health, marital adjustment, etc. may contribute to high morale on the job whereas the existence of great gratifications outside the job may contribute to individual low morale on the job by contrast! At present we do not know how to use these latter findings.

Morale must often be distinguished from "no complaint," or "contentment." High morale encourages creativity and initiative. Contentment promotes attendance, punctuality, and observance of safety regulations. Some aspects of morale operate only negatively. For example, poor working conditions reduce morale, but the improvement of working conditions merely raises morale toward the normal. Good working conditions (in the physical sense) do not produce *high* morale!

Measuring Morale

One of the first applications of the human relations approach is morale measurement of some kind. It should be emphasized that this, and other human relations procedures, will be only "symptom treatment" if investigation is restricted to the "lower echelons" of the total organization. A business or industry is an organism—a vital, dynamic whole. The human relations approach must deal with the attitudes of *all* members of the organization—top management as well as bottom ranks. It has even been suggested that it is at the "top" that the human relations approach should *begin!* Unless top management is truly interested and wishes to practice good human relations, the implementing of any program of investigation, treatment, or maintenance will be doomed to failure.

A primary goal of any human relations program is to evaluate and raise morale for two reasons: the personal welfare of all members of the total organization, and to improve productive efficiency. A usual way to start is with a morale or attitude survey.

DAY-BY-DAY INSPECTION IS NOT ENOUGH

In some organizations, low morale is apparent even to the casual visitor who walks through the plant. In general, however, even the experienced supervisor who knows his workers well can be mistaken in his day-to-day judgments. The case at the beginning of this chapter illustrates this.

EXAMINATION OF EXISTING RECORDS

An examination of labor turnover figures, absenteeism, accident rate, waste, and other statistical data is sometimes a partial indicator of morale in a department or plant. This is dangerous on several scores, however. One is that much of this data is old. Another is that the causes underlying such data are often multiple and may have changed. Good attendance, punctuality, safety and other factors may mask what is actually poor morale.

COMMUNICATIONS SYSTEM

A rather good evaluation of what goes on in the company in a general way, can be done by a "communications audit". This means studying and analyzing rumors that are picked up through the grapevine. Another method uses quizzes. This checks how much employees know of all the information that has been given them orally or in writing. The individual who answers the questions correctly gets a reward. Another technique trains supervisors to be very conscious of communication information and routes.

QUESTIONNAIRES

General morale questionnaires are probably meaningless. Such a question as "how do you like your company?", to be answered on a five-point scale, is too vague an inquiry. An acceptable questionnaire gives a question and a choice of specific answers for each one. The objective type of questionnaire is easy to score (Alas! It is not always easy to compose). Sometimes the required answers to the objective questionnaire are "yes-no," which is a limiting factor. In any event, an obstacle is that some agency (company executive, personnel, outside consulting firm) has offered choices among *its* alternatives. This kind of questionnaire is sometimes called "strait-jacket" because it fetters and limits the respondent.

A preferred but more time-consuming type of questionnaire asks "open-ended questions," such as incomplete sentences. An example is the sentence reading, "The thing I like best about my job is ——————." Scoring or interpretation is lengthy and expensive. This type of questionnaire is called descriptive. It yields an immense amount of valuable qualitative data on employees' attitudes.

MORALE OR ATTITUDE INTERVIEWS

The direct, individual, face-to-face interview is often used in eliciting individual attitudes. Since a single interview lasts at least an hour (usually longer if it is a "depth interview" which probes unconscious attitudes and feelings), it is very expensive. It requires carefully trained interviewers, and a great deal of time. Nevertheless, some organizations prefer the interview method. You will recall that interviewing solved the puzzle that arose in the Hawthorne Plant study. In that study, all the experimental changes, good and bad, were accompanied by increased production, for no apparent reason. A lengthy series of individual interviews showed that workers were far more concerned with interpersonal job relationships than with salaries or physical working conditions.

It is important that the identity of everyone who completes such a questionnaire or is interviewed be kept confidential. Those of us who have conducted this type of survey know that employee resistance is nowhere near as great as management fears. Most workers enjoy the chance to express themselves if the investigating agency has earned their respect and trust.

Supervisors can be trained to interview subordinates periodically, and thus learn much about attitudes early enough to correct or prevent aggravating situations. Some supervisors complain that this task takes too much time, and tells them nothing they didn't already know. The facts do not support such contentions.

If duties, responsibilities, and authority are properly delegated, and if a working force functions in groups, the supervisor will do well to plan a periodic evaluation for each subordinate. Each employee should be evaluated on some standard rating form, and then be invited to go over this with his supervisor. This allows the supervisor to check the picture he has of the individual with the image that the subordinate has of himself.

In human relations training, each supervisor learns to create a permissive atmosphere. In the interview, he must accept any criticism that the employee makes. This lets the employee and supervisor know what each is thinking, and reduces the possibility of misunderstanding.

As we pointed out previously, good human relations stems from the highest person in the organization down to the lowest. Each person at every level should be interviewed periodically by the person to whom he is responsible. This should show top management what things people at all levels are thinking about, and what they consider important as far as policies and other matters are concerned.

Obviously, some people have rather set attitudes. They find criticism of their pet ideas or projects very difficult to take. Human relations training, therefore, should also make each person sensitive in regard to other people. Where an individual knows that his superior (or subordinate) has a particular attitude, he should try to understand why that attitude exists, and then try to devise ways to make him receptive to criticism. (Chapter V. of personality and individual needs will consider causes of rigid attitudes.)

It is also important to realize that such interviewing gives people a rather good knowledge of other people. This should give insight into the motivating forces of these individuals. Such knowledge will lead to the best possible use of each employee in terms of the total organization. This means using data to bring about *satisfaction* to the employee, not in terms of exploitation.

A basic tenet of human relations is that a supervisor is responsible for helping the growth and development of his subordinates. The periodic evaluation interview sometimes reveals employees who can make a greater contribution to other departments than they are able to make in the jobs they hold at the time of the interview.

Summary

It is obvious that the vice-president and personnel director of the Cestus Manufacturing Company were completely ignorant of their employees' attitudes and thinking. Apparently the vacation schedule triggered off feelings and attitudes the employees already had toward management.

Because some action in management was all right in the past does not mean it will be acceptable in the future. An organization is a dynamic ongoing process. Those in charge of the organization must use every possible means to know what goes on. Because an individual "feels all right" does not mean that he should neglect to have a check-up with the family physician. Similarly, because the employee is not making trouble at the moment does not mean he isn't contemplating organizing two or three of his fellow workers for a slow-down or a quiet period. His morale requires regular evaluation.

CHAPTER FOUR

Motivation

"I hear Joe Garfield is leaving and going to work for a company in Boston. I don't get it. He's been with Lexo 12 years and makes good money as assistant superintendent. He won't make any more than he does right now. I just don't get it."

Because I interviewed Joe, I "get it." He grew up in Boston; so did his wife. His mother, now a widow, still lives there. Joe began college, going nights, after he left the Army. He wants to finish his college work and get his degree. His new company's office is just outside Boston. The firm plans to expand in New England, but only in New England. This means Joe will not have to move again as he did twice for Lexo, and as Lexo has been suggesting he do for a third time. These are some of the reasons which motivate Joe. Furthermore, Joe saw this move back to Boston as a challenge, for in Boston he felt he would have a greater opportunity to use his ability.

There is always the question—why do people work, anyway? Why do people labor over crossword puzzles for which they get no pay? Why does a next-door neighbor break his back working in his big garden when he could choose to have a small garden, or hire someone to do the heavy work? What are the forces that make a human being function? What motivates him?

We know that fundamentally we all "work to eat," but we also know that observation is an over-simplification. It does not explain why the individual takes one job rather than another, why he works hard in one setting but slackens in another. In order to understand people and to be able to help them to cooperate and be happy, we have to know what motivates them—what "makes them tick."

Needs

All people have basic biological needs—for oxygen, food, fluids, activity, rest, warmth, freedom from pain— to be able to go toward that which is biologically beneficial and avoid that which is harmful to the body. These needs are fulfilled for us by others in childhood, but as adults we must fulfill them ourselves. However, a recognition of the biological needs of Joe, cited in the introductory paragraph, does not tell us why he chooses to go to Boston rather than Lexo—both places offer a "meal ticket."

As human beings grow from infancy, and become socialized, they develop a system of secondary needs often called the psychological needs. These may be classified in various ways. One useful system considers them under the need for security, the need for belonging, the need for recognition, or the need for new experience. These needs *must* be fulfilled. To satisfy them we are driven into action. We set goals which we hope to achieve. Sometimes we can go directly toward our goal. When some obstacle or set of circumstances blocks our attainment of a goal we are frustrated. Sometimes we deal with the frustration by retreat, sometimes we "take the long way round," and sometimes we are inactive and apathetic.

Goals

The basic condition which each of us seeks is freedom from the tension that results from frustration of needs. Like everything in nature, *we* strive to achieve equilibrium, or a condition of balance, so that we feel neither an aching need for something nor an overwhelming surfeit of anything. Depending upon our past experience, each of us selects his goals in different ways. Some people feel that if they "only had money enough" everything would be wonderful. Others feel satisfaction only when they have everything their own way and can dominate others. There are people who feel it is important to be liked by everyone, and who spend all their time trying to please their associates. Very often the individual does not know what needs drive him toward a specific goal, nor does he always understand what that goal is. People may even want opposite things at the same time. One such common experience is that of wanting the satisfaction to be enjoyed from the completion of a task, while at the same time wishing to be free of the exertion of undertaking that task!

39

Looking at *other* people's goals, we see clearly that money alone does not bring freedom from other problems, nor does a position of prestige and eminence, nor does domination of others. About our *own* goals we are less clear!

This problem of the ambiguity of goals can be understood by a very simple illustration—the coffee break in industry. The custom began as a response to the need for food in an individual who had no breakfast. Today's coffee break has become a social function. It fulfills learned psychological needs.

The basic need for the coffee break began when we were children who dropped in at a playmate's home for a cookie and glass of milk. This hospitality represented recognition, security, and a strong feeling of belonging. The present-day coffee break fulfills these same needs in adults. It has so little to do with hunger or thirst that some people throng to the coffee party, but take no food or drink at all! We can see, from this, that the manager who considers the coffee break to be wasted time, and offers a food concentrate free of charge to his employees at their jobs, will encounter disdain and lack of cooperation!

We learn our goals—what to want and how to achieve it. People in different cultures satisfy their wants in different ways. (For example, some prefer hamburgers; others, raw seal meat.) However, people in a particular geographic area or culture have many common goals. We can predict generally acceptable ways of satisfying hunger, thirst, and other biological needs among most Americans. When it comes to predicting the psychological goals, however, the picture is not so clear.

The Outmoded Dollar Theory

Before the growth of unionism and social legislation of various sorts, money was the principal motivation of human behavior in business and industry. People were primarily motivated by economic factors—pay and avoidance of layoff. This is no longer the case for most of our population. The dollar-incentive is taken for granted. The manager who feels that the answer to all personnel problems is "more money" is in for a rude awakening.

Krakauer[1] describes a device he used to teach this to some of his personnel. When the employees picked up their checks, he reprimanded them for some alleged shortcomings in their work. Their shock and dismay taught them better than any barrage of words that they, themselves, were working not only for money but for recognition, approval, and esteem.

Many people work for more than mere dollars. They are often people of emotional maturity and considerable capacity, who set reasonable goals for themselves. They consider their lives to be extremely satisfying. They find they have resources within themselves which give a feeling of security. They can meet each day's challenge as it arrives. They are able to have strong relationships with members of their family and with their associates at work. They like to try new things. From their endeavors they get recognition from those close to them. They feel that this is enough.

[1] Krakauer, Daniel, "Worker Psychology, A Formula That Works," *Factory Management and Maintenance*, August, 1952.

Joe, the individual mentioned at the beginning of this chapter, is one of these people. He likes the feeling of confidence that he can do a challenging job. He has a strong feeling of belonging within his family. All he wants further is a reasonable amount of recognition. He is not particularly interested in money, as long as he has enough of it so that his family can get along "comfortably". Also, he has no desire to rise high in an organization as long as his work enables him to express his potential.

Many people are in jobs where the "psychic income" is more important to them than actual earnings. As long as they have sufficient money to satisfy the basic biological needs, they are happy if the job fulfills their learned needs. Enjoyment of new experience is important to others. Some people get immense satisfaction from trying to make the world a better place, or trying to understand and help others. Professional people find their activities satisfying in this way. It often surprises business when a Ph.D. in professional life turns down a business opportunity which pays two or three times as much!

Proponents of the dollar-theory of human motivation sometimes point to the "greed" of employees as evidence of the truth of their assertion. Oddly enough, exorbitant financial demands often indicate that *psychic* rewards are actually desired. Some people work at jobs which may involve pleasant working conditions, yet the job itself is not satisfying. They may even be bored, or frustrated, by the lack of challenge. These people will continue in such a job *only if* the salary rewards are high enough to buy them prestige, or increase the opportunity for gratification through their recreational interests or other means.

An illustration that money in itself is seldom an important motivation is the willingness of high salaried business men to leave their business affiliations for the challenges of government wartime service at a dollar a year!

The Human Relations Approach to Needs

In our materialistic society, far too many people hope for satisfaction through acquiring material things, accumulating money, or attaining authority, prestige, and status, while their psychological needs go unfulfilled. This causes emotional bankruptcy of personnel and a host of employee problems. Human relations has a responsibility to know the individual's real needs, and to help him to obtain psychic rewards, as well as pay, from his work.

If human psychological needs are learned, and thus are unique in the individual, and furthermore are often not conscious, *how* do we help the worker to recognize and satisfy them? The best method is through interviewing, particularly the depth interview. Interviews which "get at" unconscious feelings and attitudes are most fruitful.

The individual needs help in sorting out his ideas and learning what he really wants for himself. Advertising, propaganda, and unsound education have bombarded him with so many false goals and ideals that he accepts such ideas ready-made and lets them obscure his own fundamental needs. The writer recalls a case that illustrates this confusion. A student wrote a letter to his professor after graduation, eulogizing the girl he was going to marry. Six months later, a letter came saying he had decided not to marry, but to buy a car, instead!

Not all of us can be "depth interviewers"—in fact, this skill requires special training. Most managers, however, can come to understand the basic needs, wants, and goal strivings of the people for whom they are responsible. They must have patience and be willing to observe and listen. This sounds easy, but is actually very difficult and takes practice. You might, in some purely social situation, try keeping quiet and listening while some friend "beefs" about something regarding his job. You will often discover a strong impulse on your part to argue, or even worse, to advise. You will almost certainly discover how difficult it is to be quiet. If you can succeed in a prolonged period of pure listening, you will find that you'll learn a lot about your friend which long acquaintance had not taught you earlier! This emphasis upon listening can hardly be over-stressed. When in doubt, the manager should "stop, look, and listen!"

Because human beings are always changing, the manager will need to be continually observant. He must use empathy, that ability to feel oneself part of the life-situation of another. We cannot live other people's lives, but we can feel how they are living them. An illustration is the change in personality needs which comes with age. Goals change, as people grow older. New experience and personal recognition are very important to young people. In the teens you wanted to try new things —you wanted your yearbook full of signatures. In adult life there comes a shift in goals. Security, rather than new experience, becomes important. There may be frustration and self-doubt in the middle years: "Did I choose the right job—now it's too late to change. Did I marry the right person?" The individual is trying to sort out his values. As the individual grows older, the needs for "belonging" and security are the driving motivational forces. We often see how threatened the older worker is by a reorganization which he does not understand.

There are all kinds of differences among individuals which we can recognize by careful observation. Some of these are due to sex, physical makeup, intelligence and skills, differences in education, vocational training, and family upbringing. An important thing to notice about any employee is whether he is more interested in intellectual or emotional goals. The intellectual need not be a genius, but he is interested in long-range goals. He is willing to plan and accept frustrations en route to his important, and distant goal. On the other hand, the highly emotional person lives for the moment. He may have his feelings hurt, he may "blow his stack," and he often behaves in a "short-sighted" way to achieve immediate satisfaction.

When we recognize the goals which some workers have set for themselves, it shocks us to find that, one goal achieved, the individual is off and away, pushing towards another! This is the essence of the human being —he is always seeking goals. The dog fills his belly, buries a bone, and lies down in the sun to sleep and dream. But man "brings home the bacon," puts it in the refrigerator, and starts building a barbecue in his back yard!

Employee Motives

A number of things motivate employees. Calhoon and Kirkpatrick[2] cite the following:

1) *job satisfactions,* including pay, benefits, security, promotion opportunity, health and safety, sound operations, good personal treatment, and pleasant work

2) *social satisfactions,* including companionship, recognition, status, approval, and conformity

3) *Personal satisfactions,* including recognition, competition, superiority, possessiveness, being needed, welfare of the employee's family

The old concept that people worked only for money is obviously obsolete. The widely held belief that people will do the minimum amount of work for the most possible money is also open to attack. Far from avoiding work, most human beings take on all sorts of obligations which yield no money at all. People are gregarious; the social motive is very important. The amount of "joining" shows this. College fraternities, neighborhood clubs, professional and business societies, recreational groups, countless other organizations are evidence that man is

[2] Calhoon, Richard P., and Kirkpatrick, C. A., *Influencing Employee Behavior,* McGraw-Hill Book Company, 1956.

46

willing and eager to work, without thought of financial reward. The individual who does not attain status in his job may acquire it through community, church, or social activity. If he does not become a formal leader, he may be an informal leader, as we discuss in the chapter on Leadership.

It is interesting that, by and large, many people do not like change. Once they have formed into a group, they do not like to be forced to become part of another group. This presents a special problem in dealing with subordinates. Very often, both the formal and informal groups have set standards of behavior for themselves. They frequently may not realize this, but the behavior of such groups shows certain patterns. Among these patterns are the group leadership, the meeting place, the times of coming together, the type of records or communications the group uses.

Group membership gives a sense of belonging which many individuals need for psychological security. Often, group members will be extremely loyal to the group, even to the detriment of the group itself and to themselves as individuals. Group pressure can be extremely strong on individuals. "Rate breaking" problems are examples of such group pressures. Sometimes groups will endure great physical or social danger to maintain themselves. The early days of union strike strife showed some strikers were willing to endure physical hurt and family disapproval in their loyalty to the group. Supervisors must remember the strong motivation inherent in group membership. Groups may be managed satisfactorily if one knows what their standards are, and what the needs are of the members of the group, together and singly.

Supervisor's Role

In summary, then, good human relations depends upon the supervisor's knowledge of the people for whom he is responsible. He comes to understand the psychological needs they have developed, the wants they have, and the goals they are trying to reach. He is aware of changes in the individual's life which will cause changes in the individual's point of view. He will be aware of the individual's effect on the group, and *vice versa*. If he will frequently "stop, look, and listen" he will come to understand the motivations of his personnel and will be able to exert his authority in the most appropriate way. Furthermore, he will know the capacity and driving forces in each of his subordinates and associates, so that he can influence each in the way which is good for the individual, the group, and the total organization.

CHAPTER FIVE

Personality

A Typical Personality Problem

Frank Hendricks, 45-year-old Chief of Research, sat staring gloomily out of his office window. He had "blown his stack" again, and that wasn't at all good. He had thought himself under control lately. This was the first upset in a year and a half. As a scientist, he had tried to be objective about things—to take time to weigh the pro's and con's. Most of the time he succeeded. He'd plan ahead, and try to see how things were going. Then, if things seemed to be heading for a blow, he could plan ahead and "shorten sail." The sudden, unpredictable storms were what upset him.

Bill Wilkins had just dusted up a real squall. Bill, as Safety Engineer, was a dynamic personality who was all over the place at all times of day or night. He never pulled punches. He told anyone and everyone exactly what he thought in clear, direct terms. Unfortunately, Bill was apt to go off first, and think about it later. Yet, he was a most effective safety man, as the plant's remarkable freedom from accidents demonstrated.

Frank slowly cooled off and reflected on what had just happened. He and Tom Lawson, one of the most original men in the Research Department, had picked up some new ideas at a meeting in Chicago. Tom was particularly enthused about one idea, and talked about it a good bit on the way home. Frank had encouraged him. As they parted company, Tom had said, "I hope it's all right with you if I work on this idea over the weekend. Frank thought Tom meant he would work on the project at home. "Sure," he replied, "go ahead, and we'll get together for lunch Monday and see what you've come up with." But actually, Tom was asking whether he could work at the lab in the plant over the weekend. At the time, this meaning had not entered Frank's head.

Bill, the Safety Engineer, barged in unexpectedly on Monday morning and "let him have it with both barrels."

"What the hell right have you to authorize one of your stooges to endanger this whole damn plant on a Sunday? You research people think you're God's gift to this outfit . . ."

Frank tried to remain calm and to explain, but he could feel his blood pressure rising as Bill continued his tirade. After all, he'd been away a week, had a desk full of work and didn't appreciate a "chewing out" the first thing on Monday morning. He knew Bill to be a tactless fellow, and over-conscientious. When Bill stopped for breath, he said, "I'm sorry, Bill, I was away all last week and have no idea what you're talking about."

Bill came back with, "You know damn well what I'm talking about, and don't try and push it off on somebody else. Why don't you guys face up to things and deal with reality instead of a lot of blue sky? It's all your personal fault and when things like this happen—*I'm* not going to take the blame. When you OK a thing like that, you're crazy and you know it. It's just chance I found out and just luck we're all here and able to work today. You and your stooges may be geniuses and all that, but as far as I'm concerned you're all screwballs and don't give a damn about anyone but yourselves."

Frank blew up and ordered Bill from his office. He wasn't going to take that kind of thing from anybody.

"Okay!" Bill bellowed as he slammed out. "I'm leaving, but you can bet I have my eye on your pal, Lawson, and if he pulls anything like he pulled yesterday, I'm going to get him, and you, too!"

After the stormy departure, Frank sat thinking about it all. That last remark was the clue. He hadn't realized that he had given Tom what could be interpreted as permission to work in the laboratory on Sunday. Apparently Tom thought Frank had given him "carte blanche" to go ahead with his ideas.

Well, the damage was done. He must get himself organized now, and appraise its extent. He'd have to calm down, get hold of Tom, and find out what really happened. Then, he would have to plan how to make his peace with Bill. So much time and energy would be wasted. He felt as if he'd "done a week's work" in the last few minutes. He must learn not to lose his temper.

Personality Development

Apparently, Frank had discovered, during his growing up, that he tended to be somewhat emotional. He had tried to deal with this early in life by training himself to be as objective as possible. He had become an idea-man rather than a man of action. He fulfilled his needs by getting recognition for his ideas and in investigating problems in his quest for new experiences. He found he could "belong" among people who admired his ideas. He also realized that people like himself, who were idea-men, had the security of being needed by others. Frank tried to channel his physical and psychological energy into his creative world, and most of the time he succeeded. This was a constructive approach, but underlying it was the constant danger of an explosion or loss of control. The outburst of temper was based on the threat to Frank's feelings of security and the fear that this produced. Fear results from intense frustration, when the tormented person is in a dilemma and does not know what action to take.

Frank had always tried to plan ahead in order to "feel secure." Although it is unfortunate that he lost his temper, the provocation was great. Frank has the capacity to sit back and evaluate situations and plan again. He could have sulked and blamed either Tom or Bill for the situation. He might have spent time in fantasy, imagining ways of "getting even" or "fixing that so-and-so" or defending himself in other ways. Frank's personality is "pretty well put together" and his loss of control was only temporary. Some personalities do not make such a rapid recovery to stress.

Let us, then, consider the development of personality to understand some of the variations among people. The term is very difficult to define. It does *not* mean charm, or attractive appearance although these may be aspects of some personalities. Personality is the total of physical, mental, and emotional make-up of an individual as they are brought into play during his adjustments to daily life on the basis of his past experience. This is a long, and a dynamic definition. It emphasizes change. We are not exactly the same people we were yesterday, because new experience has changed us in some ways.

If one subscribes to this point of view, it is obviously futile to try to "classify people into pigeonholes." Although, for convenience, we may say that "so-and-so is one of those touchy personalities" or another person is an "extraverted personality" these statements must always carry the awareness of the uniqueness of the personality being described.

Although the personality is dynamic, we must also recognize that the unique combination of traits usually remains basically the same throughout life. The foundation of personality is built in the first four or five years of life, as the young individual learns to get along in the family and with his playmates and people in the community. Each person develops ways of meeting his needs in the kind of environment in which he finds himself. Although it is possible to modify one's personality, in actual practice most people remain substantially the same. Even those people who experience psychological counseling, psychotherapy, or psychoanalysis retain

53

their basic personality structure. They are taught to develop insight or self-understanding about their needs and to find socially acceptable means of fulfilling them.

The Dynamics of Personality

A useful way of looking at personality development is to consider the human infant. At the onset the child is self-centered. He behaves as if he expects all his biological needs to be attended to. This behavior is unconscious, and seems to be born in him. This part of personality has been called the "Id." It consists of unconscious appetites and desires for immediate gratification. As the child matures he begins to develop another aspect of personality called the "Super-Ego." This is his conscience and his value system of what is "right and wrong." He learns his standards from others, quite unconsciously. We have often overheard a child admonishing his playmates, "That's bad. It's bad to take things." Investigation would reveal the child has no true understanding of how he acquired this idea, or what it means. The final aspect of personality to develop has been called the Ego. This is the conscious, reflective, choosing part of the personality.

The Ego keeps the personality in balance so that neither Id-impulses nor Super-Ego values totally rule the personality. It is the Id which keeps us in bed late on a work day, gratifying the biological need for rest and comfort and warmth. It is the Super-Ego which says, "You ought to get up." It is the Ego which decided, "I shall get up—I am getting up"! Daily life involves many "quarrels" between Id and Super-Ego. When the Id and Super-Ego "want" different things, and the individual would like to do both, but doing both alternatives is impossible, he experiences emotional tension. When he can not "make up his mind" (reach a conscious Ego decision) we say he is being neurotic. Obviously, all people are neurotic some of the time. This does not necessarily make them candidates for a "bug doctor."

It is important that every individual realize that conflict between Id-directed and Super-Ego-directed alternatives can be solved at the intellectual, rational, or Ego-level. The adult human being can consciously evaluate his alternative goals, reflect on the possible social consequences of certain behavior, and make a choice. To do so, of course, requires that he have good insight. Once having made a decision and carried it out, he re-evaluates, "gets a feedback" and "checks his self-image." It is very important that one observe his behavior in relation to others.

EGO-DEFENSES

Sometimes, when an individual is confronted with two opposite and equally attractive ways of behaving, or two incompatible ways, he defends himself and his personal image by using certain devices for "kidding" himself. A few of the commoner ones will be discussed here. An awareness of these ego-defenses is most valuable to the manager for understanding *himself*, as well as his associates, and subordinates.

Rationalization.   Unconsciously assigning a reason for behavior but not the *real* reason. Rationalization is a way of by-passing the Ego. An example is the purchase of a new automobile, which the buyer can ill afford. He states that it is cheaper to buy a new car than to pay repair bills on the old one. His Id wants to show off with a new car but his Super-Ego says he should not go into debt. Rationalization is a widely-used defence.

Projection. Unconsciously blaming persons or things outside of ourselves for our faults or errors. The golfer blames the bad balance of his club for his slice, the typist blames her errors on a defective machine, the head of the production department blames his low output on suppliers or other departments within the plant. We all use projection frequently. The person who is *never* wrong uses it too frequently!

Repression. Not allowing bad impulses to reach consciousness. Slips of the tongue, outbursts of temper, or dreams often reveal repression. The resentful employee has a nightmare in which he is killing his superior. The "nice person" under anesthesia in the hospital uses a vocabulary he doesn't know he possesses. An angry mother screams at her beloved child, "I could kill you for doing that!"

Suppression. We make ourselves "forget" something humiliating or unpleasant. Many an adult has forgotten the time he was caught stealing in the "Five and Ten." We forget unpleasant appointments and duties. The individual who hates military service refuses to talk about his experiences. The applicant for a job "forgets" to put down the record of the time he was fired.

Fantasy. This is conscious or unconscious daydreaming in which the world is re-made to avoid unpleasant decision-making while attaining a make-believe gratification. Many people avoid action by day-dreaming such situations as "telling-off the boss," dreaming that promotion, acclaim, and great adulation have come to them, or that they are on a desert island, free from responsibility. Excessive day-dreaming which is also a substitute for activity is very unhealthy. But the kind of day-dreaming which results in actions to make the dream come true is worthwhile. We call it ambition.

Sublimation. The thing which we should like to do is improper, impossible, or forbidden, so we try to fulfill the same kind of need in a socially-approved way. For example, instead of killing the boss, we may gossip or speak of him sarcastically. We would like to punch somebody in the nose, but we go to the "gym" instead for our punching. In World War II, pin-up pictures were sublimations of the desire to have a girl.

Compensation. This device helps us to "make up for" a real or an imaginary defect. We strengthen the personality in some other area, as a rule. Thus, some inefficient people "turn on the charm." Some small and weak men are tyrants in the office. (It is interesting to note that most dictators have been men of extremely small stature.) The girl whose face is homely may accentuate her good figure. The individual whose speech is imperfect may delight in writing many office memos.

Fixation. The individual has failed to grow up emotionally. In ordinary emotional maturing we pass through the emotional states of self-love in infancy, filial love in early childhood, love for playmates in later childhood, love for persons of the opposite sex in early adulthood, and love for other human beings and unselfish love in later adulthood. Some individuals "get stuck" at one of these levels and fail to progress emotionally. We all know the "grown-up little boy" who has to have everything his own way. We also know the overly dependent employee who must ask a supervisor for approval of every detail of his work, as if that supervisor were a parent he had to please.

Regression. This device represents the unconscious return to a kind of emotional behavior which belongs to an earlier age. Regression is used when an individual feels threatened with a new situation in which he does not know how to behave. The grown woman who weeps in public when her car stalls, the adult man who has a temper-tantrum at work, and the "horseplay" at large conventions are common examples of regression.

Displacement. Unconsciously putting energy into an area other than that which has aroused emotion. A hen-pecked husband may berate his subordinates instead of his wife. An individual with a lot of unexpressed anger in him may drive belligerently, using his car like a weapon of offense.

Identification. Unconsciously making a person or thing *outside* of oneself *part* of oneself. If a fellow employee receives a nasty reprimand from the boss and you feel as angry as if you had been reprimanded yourself, this is identification. We identify with our family members. So if we see one of them in discomfort while making a public address, *we* feel uncomfortable. A secretary may identify so strongly with her boss and his need for privacy that she refuses to admit visitors. The workers in the Western Electric Hawthorne Plant study identified with their department, and the production level of the experimental group. In business and industry we try to build up identification through "house organs," news releases, and "pep meetings." Identification is healthy if it is not carried to extremes. If a mother "lives" through her daughter's career, or an executive makes "the job" his whole life, the identification is excessive. Each of us is an individual in his own right, and must not lose his own personality in that of another.

Illness. Some kinds of illnesses are due to emotional rather than physical causes. They represent punishments of the personality, or forms of escape from responsibility. They are not to be confused with conscious deception, usually called malingering. Some types of allergies, headaches, insomnia, menstrual troubles, digestive upsets, rashes, and high blood pressure are caused in some people by strong emotional frustration. A common example of such an illness is the Monday morning sickness of a child who hates school. He actually "throws up" or "runs a temperature" until the time for school is past. We all know that some kinds of ulcers are associated with the stress of modern life for some individuals. Many people have heart symptoms which frighten them and for which no physical basis can be found.

A change of job, or transfer to another department, away from a frustrating situation, often relieves such distress. Illness is an ideal way for some people to solve their problems because by being ill one receives sympathetic attention, is free from responsibility, and can get well when it is convenient. Before the advent of so much automation, many of us can remember the billing clerk who always seemed to get a bad migraine attack at the busy billing time. Many of us can recall a time when

59

we had an important examination, interview, or public speech confronting us and had to make a dozen trips to the bathroom the hour before the ordeal. We are well familiar with the sleeplessness that occurs the night be-fore an important meeting. In a host of ways we have evidence that in ourselves, our workers, and our associ-ates the bodily equilibrium can be upset by emotional stress. Some people carry on during such periods of stress and eventually learn how to minimize stress but other people succumb to illness as an escape.

Under illness we might well consider alcoholic addic-tion as an example of escape. The problem of alcohol and the worker is a great one. The true alcoholic is not a person who drinks a very large amount of liquor so much as he is a person who drinks to give himself cour-age, or to help him to forget his problems. The problem drinker in business and industry is one who *must* drink in order to face the problems of living. He is quite a different proposition from the individual who has com-mitted an indiscretion from time to time, by drinking too much in a social situation, for example.

Summary

In this chapter we have had a short course in the psy-chology of personality. We have seen that the structure of personality is unique to each individual and depends partly upon his biology, his mentality, his emotional make-up, and his training as he has experienced the problems of living. We have seen that within each per-sonality there is going on all the time a striving for equilibrium between the force we call the "Id" and the aspect of personality named the Super-Ego. It has been pointed out that the Ego—the rational part of the personality, consciously makes choices among alternatives of behavior. In situations where the choices are conflicting, or unclear, we have shown that the individual becomes indecisive and we have called such behavior neurotic. We have shown a number of devices or techniques by which the individual "kids himself" in order to protect his Ego and preserve his self-image. From a consideration of the Ego defenses we undoubtedly discovered descriptions of our own behavior and illumination respecting the behavior of others.

Let's return to the situation described at the beginning of the chapter. We can see that Frank has *suppressed* his anger most of the time. He showed *regression* when he ordered Bill from his office. Some *illness* was revealed by his feelings of a rise in blood pressure during the incident.

Regarding Bill, we notice *projection*—he is quick to blame Frank without waiting for an explanation. He may be using *displacement* with his invectives about Frank and his stooges—perhaps he is angry about something unrelated to Frank. He seems to feel inferior by his use of the term "genius"; he is expressing this by *compensation,* his rough talk to Frank. Bill is emotionally immature and probably *fixated* at the childhood level of playmates and fighting.

We might hazard a guess as to how Frank will need to deal with Bill, once he himself has "cooled off". He will undoubtedly use the interview method, in which he listens and lets Bill "let off steam" and express his feelings fully. After this, he will probably sympathize with Bill's point of view, and apologize for the misunderstanding about Tom. (He will not project—"pass the buck" or blame Tom, since he himself is at fault.)

Having had his opportunity to express his resentment, probably Bill in turn will be able to let his Ego rather than his Id deal with the situation. He will probably apologize for "blowing his top" and both will part in a friendly way. Frank's knowledge of the dynamics of personality will help him to establish a better working situation with Bill. It should also assist him in dealing with the talented but impetuous Tom.

A caution is desirable here. In the account of the Human Relations point of view Frank will take in handling Bill, it is important to see that what is being utilized is an understanding of personality needs rather than a technique or "gimmick" for manipulation. Let us suppose we use a technique without understanding, and tell Bill to "get it off his chest" so we can "get down to brass tacks and settle this." Such an approach will arouse his resentment instead of his cooperation. It fails to take into account that Bill *needs* to express himself. It ignores the recognition of *when Bill is relaxed* and reasonable because he has expressed himself. Bill is not "a case" but a human personality. He must be treated that way. Gimmicks are not enough.[1]

[1] An interesting work on the dynamics of personality, written by an engineer who has taught human relations, is an older book, now out of print, but available in most public libraries. Magoun, F. Alexander, *Balanced Personality*, Harper & Bros., 1947.

CHAPTER SIX

Communication

A Typical Problem in Poor Communication

At 9:30 on a Monday morning, Fred Stanton, Chief Engineer, picked up his phone and dialed the number of one of his staff. He received no answer. Turning to his secretary, he said, "Dial all of those guys and locate them for me. There are a couple of things I have to talk to them about this morning." He sat back and began to mull over the ideas he wanted to present to his staff.

The company had just moved into new, but already crowded, quarters. Stanton had a fairly large office to himself and his secretary. Each of his five engineers under him had a private cubicle. Down the hall from Stanton's office was a conference room. Here, coffee was served from 10 to 12, and was available at 15-minute intervals to the various departments of the company. The time for the engineering staff was 10:00 a.m. "Perhaps they're at coffee," said his secretary.

"Maybe they are," he replied, "but they're not supposed to be. I'll go and see." He did so, and found the conference room deserted. He looked in each of the five cubicles but could find none of his men. He met the head of the production department and asked if he'd seen them.

"Sure," was the answer. "They're down in the men's 'john' having coffee."

Scarcely believing his ears, Stanton went down to the men's lavatory and opened the door. He saw five men sitting on window sills, wash bowls, and the rubbish can, smoking, drinking coffee, and engrossed in talk. Nobody noticed him. He turned around and walked out, furious. His first inclination was to chew them out, and perhaps fire them all. He knew this was silly, however. They were good men whom he'd picked himself, and would be hard to replace. On the other hand, he felt they were abusing their privileges.

"Why in Hell," he thought, "should they be in the 'john' drinking coffee at 9:30 on a Monday morning, when at 10:00 they could have their coffee in the comfort of the conference room!"

Back in his office, he raged. "Marge, take this note to each of my men. The lousy stinkers—I'm going to do something about this."

Within 10 minutes, he had all five engineers on the carpet. But he got this answer from Bill West, one of the engineers:

"The men's room is the only place where we can get together and talk. The cubicles are too small to hold all of us at the same time. We took our coffee to the men's room in case our talk runs over fifteen minutes and we should hold up the next group in the conference room. We hoped when we came into the new building the engineering department would have a place where it could meet as a group."

The foregoing situation illustrates the one basic aspect required for communication to take place, namely, an *opportunity* for communication. This opportunity is absent in the Engineering Department of the company at the present time.

Communication is the process of passing information and meaning from one or more persons to one or more persons. Notice that a minimum of two persons is always involved. If you are alone in a room, listening to a tiresome commercial on the radio, and you make a raspberry noise at the announcer, you are not communicating—you are merely expressing yourself.

Two-Way Communication

We cannot over-emphasize the importance of the two-person aspect of communication. If you dispatch an important memorandum to your staff, you cannot conclude that the mere distribution of that memorandum makes it a communication. The memo must be received, read, and understood in order to be a communication! It is important to ensure that communications "get through." The best way to check this is by the process of "feedback." This refers to the report which the sender obtains, which indicates his message has been received. Feedback is present when the mother asks her child, "Now tell me, dear, what I told you to get at the store." Feedback in business and industry may come directly, through questionnaires or morale surveys, from evidence that instructions were carried out, from gossip, and from such situations as Fred's talk with Bill in the foregoing situation.

All job-oriented communication in business and industry has two primary goals. The first is to give people information and understanding so they *can* work together. The second is to supply information and understanding which will motivate people so that they *will* work together.

Factors in Communication

Most of our communication is with symbols—pictures, sounds, or other sensory images which represent objects which are not present, or which represent ideas. The letters and sounds of a language are symbols. Mathematical formulae are symbols. Drawings, blueprints, charts, and diagrams are symbols. We have already referred to status symbols such as the kinds of rugs in offices of executives. Man is the only creature who communicates by symbols.

VERBALIZATION

In dealing with language, we refer to verbalization, or the use of words. This unique ability of man is acquired in the process of growing up. Language ability develops in four steps—hearing words, speaking words, reading words, and writing them. The human brain has the amazing capacity of integrating these four types of experience. Inasmuch as each individual is a unique

66

personality, however, born with different equipment and having different experiences in the process of living, there are individual differences in his mastery of these four aspects of language development. There are people who are not "bright enough" to master vocabulary beyond a certain level, and there are those who are bright enough but who lack sufficient education. Others may come from a foreign language background and find communication difficult. This is an important problem in today's European Common Market. An example is a firm located in Belgium where all the technical specifications are in German, the language of the parent company. The Belgiums speak Flemish (a kind of Dutch) or Walloon (a kind of French). Confronted with German of a technical sort, they have great difficulty in understanding the specifications.

SEMANTICS

Semantics is the science of the meanings of words. We know that the dictionary gives several, often dozens, of meanings for a single word. In addition to these, words often have particular meanings for individuals or groups of persons. A plant manager once posted a notice reading: "There will be no playing of the nigger pool during working hours." Almost immediately, three negro employees came into his office and protested. They understood the allusion perfectly well, but resented it. The manager was very surprised. He stated that negroes themselves referred to betting on U.S. Treasury balances as "the nigger pool." The emotional tone attached to certain words varies from culture to culture. It is important for the speaker or writer to know this and utilize emotionally-toned words to enhance communication rather than to arouse antagonism.

SENSORY DIFFERENCES

Differences in the ability to hear and see interfere with good communication. Some people hear well with their ears, but take longer to turn these sounds into meaning in the brain than for the normal person. In public schools today, children's ability to understand what they hear is investigated frequently. Public school systems also check visual ability at frequent intervals; they know that children's reading difficulties sometimes originate from difficulties in seeing.

MOTIVATION

Motivation also determines how well we respond to written or oral communications. After World War II, a company completed a remodeling project of one department and enclosed a notice of the transfer to the new quarters in the weekly envelope. The notice of transfer was in large type at the top of the sheet. Beneath it was a lengthy, single-spaced announcement of the new rate schedule, with an account of how these rates had been established. The following week the girls were dissatisfied with their pay. A slowdown was their reaction to what they felt was the unfairness of the new rates. After a conference of supervisors and head management, a department meeting was called. The rate-setting department explained how the new rates were set, and showed the girls that their pay would actually increase as a result of the new system. After the girls conceded that working conditions were improved and that the new pay rate seemed fair, they asked, "Why didn't you tell us this in the first place?" Apparently, they had read the transfer notice on the way home the week before—and had never read the more difficult, single-spaced material. Motivation to read closely-spaced material or fine print is usually low. (Have you, yourself, read such material in your insurance policy? I venture to predict the answer will be "No.")

We cannot communicate once, and "have it stick"—we must do it many times and in different ways. Because of widespread sensory differences, important communications should be presented in a variety of ways. For most people, vision is the preferred sense. So many of our presentations are in the form of printed material, films, pictures, posters, and the like. A substantial group of people, however, respond better to oral material. Public address announcements and oral instructions and explanations, as a supplement to visual presentations, reach such people. Where we can, we try additional means to reach those to whom we wish to communicate.

In training programs, for example, we may place a worker's hands in the desired position, so he can understand by the feelings in his muscles what we want of him. In persuading a typist to "accept" an electric typewriter, we may invite her so "sit down and try it out." Where we cannot communicate by offering a direct experience, we substitute words which evoke images of the kind of experience we are describing. Thus the advertiser writes, "So sheer that you could pass it through a wedding ring." This makes the reader think of a mass of diaphanous stuff compressed into a small area.

In showing to workers the desirability of seatbelts in cars (a procedure we hope to make compulsory for safety) we may invite them to get into a car and strap such a belt, and lean against it. They then actually experience the support and protection that such a belt can give. The wider the appeal of a communication to several senses, the more likely its understanding and acceptance.

Reading and Listening as Human Relations Training

Training in more efficient reading and listening is an important part of the human relations program of many companies. Because of the vast amount of printed communication in and outside of industry, companies offer employees training programs to improve the speed and efficiency of reading. Research and experimentation in computers and various forms of automation, as well as the great development in engineering and in the application of the behavioral sciences, has resulted in new words developing and old words acquiring new meaning. (In the course of this book you have been introduced to such a new vocabulary.)

Some companies have begun to present programs teaching people "how to listen". It is interesting to ask a friend who has listened to a news broadcast where the items were given rapidly, to tell you what the news is.

Although he may have "heard" everything that was said in the 15-minute program, he usually can produce only two or three items. He had insufficient time to relate the heard sounds to past experiences, to incubate the material, and assimilate it in a meaningful way. Today, we receive a great deal of language material by public address, tape and disk recordings, and radio. It is essential to master the process of communication. It is likewise useful to realize that although the "lecture method" can offer a great amount of information, this does *not* necessarily mean that the listeners are able to avail themselves of this.

The person who listens to a "live" lecture is stimulated not only by what he hears, but by what he experiences through other senses. This was brought home recently to the author in a situation where he gave a lecture to 300 students, using a fixed microphone. It was later reported that the smaller lectures, without microphone, were far more effective. The students missed the activity, gestures, facial expression, and other cues which were hidden by the lectern and microphone. Although the microphone made the lecture more audible, students preferred the lecturer to have freedom of movement and expression.

Gaining Attention

In communicating, it is vital that the speaker or writer gain the attention of those whom he is addressing. On the platform we may use a special tone, in a written message we may use capital letters, pictures, or a colored announcement—some device must be used. Some of us can remember President Roosevelt's "Fireside Chats" on radio. After the "burble" of the announcer, during which there might be inattentiveness and a search for cigarettes or a more comfortable chair, Roosevelt's warm voice would be heard in his opening greeting, "My friends. . . ." Regardless of one's political persuasions, that greeting made everyone attend to what Roosevelt was saying.

Securing attention is often a matter of "timing." An editorial or radio discussion of the Stock Market ordinarily arouses attention only in a specialized group—but a discussion of the Stock Market "crash" in the summer of 1962 made every adult "sit up and take notice." The theme or topic about which a communication is to be made commands or rejects attention. Thus a newspaper column headed "New Ways to Use Left-over Turkey" seldom captures the attention of male readers.

The importance of engaging the attention has carried some communicators to excesses, of course. We are all familiar with advertisements which portray a pretty girl in a minimum of clothing, while the text deals with piston rings or some other alien topic; and with the third-class mail envelope which contains a "real penny" for your thoughts, if you will fill out the enclosed invitation to try a product.

Incongruity captures the attention, but *does not sustain* it. The best way to keep attention is to relate the communication to the needs of the reader or listener. The person to whom we are addressing ourselves must be oriented promptly to the topic on which information is given or sought, so that he will not set up psychological barriers to receiving the communication. By "psychological barriers" is meant such responses as "turning a deaf ear," "closing the mind," "being against it," or characterizing the communication as "mumbo-jumbo, gobbledy-gook."

Need for Clarity

Common errors in communication include the overuse of pronouns in written and spoken sentences. Wherever possible, nouns should be used instead of pronouns. The vocabulary should be adjusted to the needs of the listener or reader. Although the writer has tried to be on guard against using an academic vocabulary in this work, undoubtedly the reader has detected a number of oversights on his part! (If you will examine the preceding sentence, you will see an example of the confusion pronouns create. Whose part is "his part"—the writer's or the reader's?)

Instructions

A special type of communication is the instruction or order. Dr. Paul Pigors, of the Massachusetts Institute of Technology, points out that every order is a communication process which should have seven specific steps:
1. Planning. *Who* will do *what?* How will the order be given?
2. Preparation. The recipient of the order must understand *why* the order is given.

73

3. Presentation. Instructions must be clear and presented in such a way as to ensure voluntary co-operation.
4. Verification. The order must be understood and the recipient must be willing to perform it.
5. Action. The order is carried out.
6. Follow-up. The effect of the action is checked.
7. Appraisal. The order is evaluated—did it fulfill its purpose and obtain results? Can there be improvement? Where? How?

Source of the Communication

The source is important in all communication, because the recipient's attitude is very much influenced by the source. Information from an authoritative source carries more weight than communications from other sources. The authoritative source may be one which holds power over the individuals receiving the communication, or it may be a source which represents special competency. An example of the first type of source is the "boss" who gives an order. If the driver of a trolley car stops and says, "All passengers out," most of us alight readily, without argument. An illustration of the authority of competency is the receipt of a bill from the income tax audit department stating an arithmetical error has been found in our return, and requesting an additional payment. We usually "believe" these experts, and pay up without scrutinizing our return to find the department's error!

Most authoritative sources are representatives of formal organization. The trolley car operator and the tax department are recognized as agents of organizations. Sometimes, however, *informal* sources may be authoritative. Thus, if our neighbor mentions that he is surveying for a new state road in our area, we become anxious lest our property be confiscated, or depreciate in value. Two department secretaries, gossiping in the cafeteria, may be overheard by a fellow employee. Because of the closeness of the secretaries to "the top," the listener may assume that what he hears is actually fact.

RUMOR AND PROPAGANDA

Communications often arise from non-authoritative sources. The secretaries referred to above may be ill-informed, malicious, extravagant and boastful. The listener who overhears their remarks may pass them on as actual facts—and thus start a rumor. Rumors often spread through the informal lines of communication referred to in Chapter Three. As mentioned there, every attempt should be made to prevent rumors, or substitute adequate information for them. The presence of a large body of rumor in an organization indicates low morale.

Propaganda is usually conceived of as communication to influence the behavior and feeling of the recipients for purely selfish purposes. It is usually a one-sided presentation carrying strong emotional appeal. A motion picture with Jack Webb which shows how a U.S. Air Force installation saves the life of a prominent citizen in a nearby community who objected to the nuisance and noise of the planes, is an example of propaganda. The laudatory leaflets enclosed with your monthly utility bills are also propaganda. Many company newspapers are propaganda, and recognized as such by employees.

Propaganda has come to be a dirty word in the United States, yet many worthy communication programs are actually propaganda. Examples are public education, where children are taught that "the American way of life" is the best way of life, and advertising. A toothpaste advertisement, with its emotional appeals, offering new flavor experiences and improved social acceptance, may be propaganda, yet it *does* encourage us to clean our teeth!

"Getting Across"

Successful communication results from necessary attitudes and techniques rather than magic. Many a manager wishes to communicate, yet unintentionally threatens the individual or group by assuming a superior or patronizing attitude. In good communication, it is important to attract attention and then to establish a psychological relationship between the parties involved.

When Fidel Castro visited Harvard shortly after becoming head of the Cuban government, he achieved this psychological relationship in a speech. He began by apologizing for his limited English, and expressed the hope he could make himself understood. He then identified himself with the students in the audience by pointing out that he, too, had attended a university. He established rapport (mutual respect and understanding) so that even those who came to heckle stayed to listen attentively.

The person who is communicating must be sensitive to the reactions of the persons to whom he is communicating. If he is face-to-face, he will listen to the inflections of the respondent's voice, the pace of his words, even to his silences. He will watch bodily and facial expression, note changes of color, breathing and other cues. From time to time, in an extensive communication, he will invite "feedback" so that he can be sure he is getting his message across. If there seems to be a block to understanding, he will try to clarify his communications *after* he has obtained reactions.

Nothing is sadder than the person who explains and explains, without understanding the needs of the one to whom the communication is addressed. An amusing example of over-explanation is the father's elaborate account to the child of the story of human birth. The child has asked, "Where was I born, Daddy?" What he really wanted to know was in what city or town!

It is often desirable to try out written communications in advance. Thus, the brochure of instructions which the engineering department has prepared to accompany a do-it-yourself furniture kit may be tried out on members of the staff, or better still, a sample of consumers. Such instructions often turn out to be unintelligible, and must be re-worked many times before the intention to communicate is fulfilled. The author has frequently advised students to read the first draft of a term paper to themselves or a friend before putting it into final form. In writing an examination, they are advised to imagine who will read the material, and under what conditions. Visualizing the instructors under pressure at examination time results in greater clarity and brevity of answers. We have already referred to this process of "putting yourself in another's place as a most valuable application of human relations. Empathy would have prevented the "boner" cited earlier, where manager put up a sign reading "No Playing the Nigger Pool!"

Channels of Communication

Equally important to *how* we say it is *where* we say it. Some years ago, the author was asked to study human relations in a hospital staff. The basic problem was that the personnel did not have a clear picture of the table of organization; consequently, the channels of communication were extremely confused. It was recommended that the assistant-director draw up a table of organization in terms of communication, to clear the bottlenecks. Although the department heads had thought they were doing a good job, their subordinates were not carrying out their specific duties. Much of the routing of communication in the hospital had been done informally by the telephone operator, who had to make judgments about where messages were to go.

Communications within an organization take three major paths: down, horizontal, and up. Communication downward usually takes the form of directives, public address announcements, notices on bulletin boards, and house organ articles. Communications up the line may come about through a *good* suggestion system, employee representation by means of committees, and by means of the periodic evaluation interviews mentioned in Chapter 3. Communication upward is traditionally through formal organization pathways. It is business etiquette that the employee does not by-pass his immediate superior and "go over his head" to the "big boss."

The prohibition against direct consultation with top management brings some problems regarding "open door policy." Some top executives pride themselves on their accessibility. In many organizations, the open door is a physical reality but a psychological myth. Where the door is truly open, some interesting situations may occur, as in the H. P. Hood & Sons Co., a milk company. The tale is that years ago a maintenance man walked into Mr. Hood's office, complaining that nobody would buy him a new broom, and wanting Mr. Hood to know this. This represents one extreme of the open door policy. In the same company, another aspect is that top management is always represented at company parties, mixing informally with employees, and giving them a chance to make complaints, suggestions, and comments.

Some years ago, a senior railroad employee was telling about workers' relationships with the president of the company. Whenever there was a party of any sort, the railroad president attended, with his wife. Frequently his wife played the piano to accompany singing employees. Meantime, said the railroad conductor, "The Old Man was having his ear bent by a bunch of guys griping about all kinds of things. He always tried to listen to all of them." This is an example of "informal open door policy." Sears Roebuck, the national mail order house, has a policy that no employee can be discharged after four years' employment without his case being reviewed by top management. The purpose of this unusual accessibility of high company officials is to avoid discharges due to "personality clash".

Horizontal communication occurs among workers of approximately the same rank, as within the same department. It is day-to-day, desk-to-desk, bench-to-bench communication.

Crossing lines and transcending the usual vertical or horizontal communication channels is a network of informal communication. Communications of members of a family may constitute such a network. Some companies so fear this type of informal communication that they have a policy against hiring relatives of current employees. Another type of informal network is social. Members of the company bowling team may have communication on business matters interspersed with their social relationships. Several persons in a company who grew up together, or who have come to the present organization from the same company, may engage in a good deal of informal communication beyond the usual formal channels.

It is management's responsibility to provide adequate communication channels. Every supervisor, and each top and middle management person, must be constantly aware of this obligation.

Subordinates, in order to develop their full potentialities must have access to necessary information, and be able, in their turn, to pass on vital data. A good way for supervisors to create a good communication relationship with and among subordinates is to counsel employees, or to make sure that someone else is doing this, by means of the periodic evaluations. Today the supervisor is responsible for far more than "getting out production" or "increasing the volume of sales"—he is responsible for the general welfare of his department and the growth of his subordinates.

COUNSELING

Counseling ordinarily refers to the use of interviews to help the individual to improve his self-understanding and master the problems of everyday living. In large companies, psychologically trained counselors are available to assist employees directly with work or personal difficulties. In many such organizations, foremen and supervisors often refer troubled or difficult workers to the counseling department. Such a department usually operates under the personnel department.

Where it is not practical to provide such a service, supervisors often counsel "on the job." The counselor's job is to provide a climate of "acceptance". The interviewee can say anything without arousing disapproval, shock, or argument. The counselor does *not* advise. He listens, and may ask questions which will develop insight in the counselee. The non-directive interview is a preferred approach, especially for the non-professional, on-the-job counselor. (The outstanding exponent of this method is Carl Rogers, of the University of Chicago.) The method, applied in the business setting, is to encourage the individual to talk freely. Thus, instead of saying to a worker, "What's eating you, Jim?" the non-directive approach says, "You're troubled, Jim, tell me about it."

When the individual "runs down," the non-directive interviewer reflects what has been said—paraphrases it briefly in such a way as to indicate his acceptance and understanding. Mostly, the non-directive non-professional counselor just listens. He shows no approval, disapproval, or judgment. He makes no promises. He "tattles no tales" to management. He shows confidence that the individual will find his own solutions. He supports and encourages the worker whom he is counseling. He does *not* play "Mr. Echo," duplicating the interviewee's remarks, nor are his own remarks limited to a perpetual "Mmh."

While the direct interview method of question and answer lends itself well to screening applicants for employment and the like, the non-directive method is *the* method for problem situations. It elicits *feelings,* which are more important than facts, in situations of emotional upset. You will understand this when you think of some occasion where you "got something off your chest" and felt the better for it, even though the aggravating situation itself had not changed. (Many a good wife is a good counselor to her troubled husband when he brings the burden of his work frustrations home to her!)[1]

[1] Two useful, readable works on interviewing and counseling are:
Cannell, Charles F., and Robert L. Kahn, *The Dynamics of Interviewing,* John Wiley & Sons, Second Printing, 1960, especially pp. 316-328.
Brammer, Lawrence M., and Everett L. Shostrom, *Therapeutic Psychology,* Prentice-Hall, 1960. This is a rather advanced work for the lay reader, but Chapter 16 is especially relevant.

PUBLIC RELATIONS

Thus far we have been discussing intra-company communication, but our account requires a consideration of "outside" communication as well. It is important that an organization build up a good image in the community. A favorable attitude in the community makes it easier to recruit employees, settle employee grievance, secure community cooperation respecting zoning, taxes, licensing, and a host of other matters. The writer remembers the situation some years ago when Lever Brothers, the soap company, relocated its office and transferred its personnel to another part of the country. Hundreds of employees had to offer their houses for sale in what became, temporarily, a highly competitive real estate market. The ill-will associated with the shock of this rather rapid removal still survives in the memory of persons in the greater Boston, Massachusetts area. This was extremely poor public relations, as well as a reducer of morale within the company.

A good way to build public relations is to encourage members of the organization to take an active part in community affairs. This may even involve allowing some time off from work in order to carry out extra community duties on occasion. An example is the release of an executive from some of his duties during an important community fund-raising campaign, such as a health drive. A good publicity program which makes available to the local press information about what the company is doing in relation to the community, and newsworthy items about its products, services, and personnel help build a good public image.

Joint community and industrial programs are another method of improving public acceptance and understanding of the business organization. Some companies encourage plant visits by school children, college students, and special groups of adults. In the writer's community the Coca-Cola company has been very hospitable in guiding girl and boy Scouts through its plant, as well as providing free Coke. This is good public relations and good merchandising going hand in hand. A factory tour may make members of the community see how much the plant is doing to abate a local smoke nuisance, or clean its waste water, or destroy odoriferous or unsightly waste products from its manufacturing processes. Finally, the economy of most communities depends partly on the businesses and industries within its borders, so that companies must assume responsibility for educating the public to an awareness of this, and building a favorable public image.

Summary

This has been a relatively long chapter for a book of this length, and yet we have hardly scratched the surface. From an everyday example of the communication difficulties of Fred Stanton, Plant Engineer, we have covered a host of topics up to communication of the organizational image to the public. We have seen that communications occur when we do not intend them, but on the other hand understanding has been absent where we hoped it had been produced. It has been emphasized that skill in communication can be developed. We have to secure attention, build a favorable attitude of interest, couch our message in terms which can be understood, invite a feedback, and constantly evaluate our progress towards improvement. The formal and informal channels of communication within an organization have been described. Awareness of informal channels has been stressed, and the need for adequate communication to prevent rumor and low morale. The reader has been invited to develop sensitivity to the reactions of others to his communications and to try to reach personnel through sight, sound, and other sensory experiences. Above all we have stressed the importance of recognizing the purpose of our communications, and planning how to obtain the desired outcome. Finally, we have endorsed the non-directive technique as a useful method, within the abilities of the non-specialist, for informal on-the-job counseling.

CHAPTER SEVEN

Leadership

Portrait of One Leader

The section heads of an insurance company's personnel department received a memo late on Tuesday, October 18. Several did not have the chance to read it until Wednesday morning. It read:

Inasmuch as I have to be on the West Coast for business on Monday and probably won't be back until the end of the week, I thought it best that we have a staff meeting this week instead of the regular one that is due next Thursday. I am sure you are all aware of several loose ends that we ought to get knitted up as soon as we possibly can; therefore, I am asking you to meet on Friday, the 21st, at 3:00 p.m. I am sure you will all feel better if we can get some of the things we have been working on wrapped up by 5:00.

Attached is an agenda which you can be thinking about before Friday so we can quickly come up with all the answers. I am sure my staff is capable

87

of dealing adequately and rapidly with all this, and I shall be looking forward to seeing you in the staff room at 3:00 p.m. on Friday.

Jack Mullins
Vice-President in charge
of Personnel

P.S. Of course we will have coffee as usual, but I think we will want to get the meeting started at 3:00; you can drink your coffee while we talk.

By 3:05 p.m. the eight members of Mullins' staff were gathered in the staff room. They discussed some of the items on the agenda, which was as follows:

1. Plan for the shift-over to electronic equipment.
   A. Training
   B. Wages and Salaries
   C. Transfers
   D. Job Evaluations
2. Suggestions for new application forms.
3. Problem of morale in Section Seven Typing Pool.
4. Replacement of Mrs. Webb, interviewer.
5. Present status of course on claims interviewing for newly-hired claims men.

At 3:30, Mullins rushed into the room breathlessly and sat down at the head of the table.

"Well, folks, here I am. I'm sorry to be late, but the Treasurer had me in his office on a rather important matter. This is sort of confidential and it's one of the reasons why I'm going out to our West Coast office to talk about this. I hope you'll just sort of keep this under your hats, but it looks as if we're going to give the employees (which includes all of us) a chance to buy up some company stock. We apparently have done rather well in the past year or so. I'm really awfully sorry to be late, but I'm sure we'll get everything cleared up.

"Now, of course this brings up one more thing we might consider today because it really belongs in our department because this stock deal will tie up with the wage and salary administration that is under you, Fred, and we'll have to talk this over. I guess maybe the best thing to do would be to wait 'til I get back and then we can, that is you and I, sit down and talk it over and then bring it up at the next staff meeting here after we suggest how we can get this thing implemented.

"Now, okay, well, I suppose we ought to get on with what we've got here today. There are quite a few items on the list here. There's always the question, of course, of where to begin. I thought of starting with some of the simpler ones like the matter of Mrs. Webb. I don't think there's too much of a problem there. It's a matter of that she's going to be leaving us soon; as you know, she's sort of in a family way and I'm not sure how long we should keep a potential mother actually in interviewing. Of course, there's the question of the attitude of people who come in to be interviewed and are interviewed by a, us, well, you know, a lady in the family way.

"Uh, I'm not sure that this makes a good impression but, uh, I think we can, uh, decide what to do with this; and I suppose there's a question of whether we should have Mrs. Webb back after her confinement.

In fact, uh, I don't know if she wants to come back. Uh, Gene, have you, uh, talked with her about this; after all, I suppose this is really in your department. You probably, uh, have been thinking this over. Well, uh, you have talked to her, Gene? Okay! Well, I don't know if we should take this up as the first item. Maybe we should.

"I guess, uh, we ought to decide perhaps the order in which these things ought to go. It looks to me as if we really had quite a bit to do here in this matter of the new electronic equipment that is coming in and the way in which we've got to get set up for that. Have any of you heard of the exact date that we've got to begin to get people on that? For some reason I haven't been informed of it; some of you might know."

The question now arises as to how competent a leader Jack Mullins actually is. Consider the memorandum, the agenda and the opening of the meeting. He is obviously well-intentioned, and perhaps in many ways a good leader. Since he has become Vice-President in charge of Personnel, it seems that he must have some leadership qualities.

Born or Made?

Many people have believed that leaders are born, not made. However, there has been some shift in this idea. Some now believe that individuals can be educated or trained to assume leadership. Others do not. *Leadership*, a 1943 publication of the Adjutant General's School Lecture Series, says:

". . . It is difficult to see how leadership can be taught. No authoritative test on the development of leadership has yet been approved by the War Department. If . . . leadership results from an emotional relationship between the leader and his followers, we may well ask ourselves whether a common trend in the Army toward stoicism and a suppression of the emotions will not defeat our purposes of stimulating leadership."

Roger Bellows, in his book on *Creative Leadership,* says very flatly, "Leaders are made, not born. Our changing times require more and better leaders. How can we get them? The answer: Train them." [1]

Notice that the terms "leader" and "leadership" are often used interchangeably. We call someone a "leader" when he influences and controls the actions of others. Since we believe we can educate or train people to carry out certain behavior patterns, it seems reasonable to expect to train individuals to behave in the way we call "leadership behavior." If this is true, then we have to assume that "leaders" can be made.

Leadership, as a behavior pattern, means activity by the person showing leadership. Behavior implies action, and output of physical energy. Some authorities believe that a person must show physical activity to exercise leadership.

Chapple and Coon, in their book *Principles of Anthropology,* write:

"A leader is a man who, when more than two persons are present, originates action on the majority of events to which those present respond." [2]

These authors believe physical energy is one aspect of a leader that may be inherited or inborn. A person with

[1] Bellows, Roger, *Creative Leadership,* Prentice-Hall, 1959.
[2] Chapple, Eliott, and Carleton S. Coon, *Principles of Anthropology,* Holt, 1942.

much physical, and perhaps psychic energy, is the one who will initiate action.

Physical appearance is another possible "inborn quality" of a leader. This depends, of course, on heredity and general health. Someone with a good build, of pleasing appearance according to our culture's standards, is one whom we may regard as an "authority figure." We may also associate pitch of voice or other mannerisms with authority traits to which we have become conditioned during our youth.

Special aptitude or capacity is another inborn aspect of a leader. Having a special talent or capacity needed for handling a given situation may make someone into a leader temporarily. For example, a group of hunters, lost in a forest, may depend on a native of the area to help them find their way out. They follow him because in this situation he has a capacity which they all lack. This shows that, regardless of innate individual abilities of appearance, the *situation* is important in determining what will occur in the way of leadership.

Types of Leaders

Leadership has been classified in many ways. The terms frequently heard are "autocratic," "democratic," and *"laissez-faire."* There are also the terms "paternalism" and "autocrat." The terms suggest their meanings; the autocrat takes all decision-making unto himself and acts in a dictatorial way. The *laissez-faire* leader is appointed or elected, but he does not take an active role.

He lets his followers do as they wish. Many leaders who consider themselves very democratic are really benevolent despots. They hear what everyone has to say, then try to manipulate the group to get their own way after all.

OTHER CLASSIFICATIONS OF LEADERS

Some individuals are extremely egocentric and exhibitionistic. In any situation, they move forward and tend to take over. This is because they have both physical and psychological energy, and in the past have been leaders. Such a person may or may not have the capability in a given situation to be a successful, acceptable leader, but he feels that he should be. One easily recognizes this sort of behavior if one thinks about some social organizations. Very often, some one who joins an organization becomes extremely active in getting elected to office. However, he may not be re-elected, since he does not function as a leader. The fact that a person has had leadership roles and is extremely dynamic does not mean that he is the best person for a leadership role in a given situation, or that he can even fill it.

The extremely gregarious person also comes to the fore frequently. He is friendly, outgoing, has a good sense of humor, and offends nobody. But this does not mean that he can lead others and help them make decisions. Elementary school class officers, chosen for popularity but lacking leadership ability, are a common example.

A third type of leader likes to control the activities of others. He likes the feeling of power, but cares nothing for individual recognition. He may sit in the background, "pull strings," and watch others carry out his wishes. He will sometimes study a situation very carefully before making any move, then exert subtle influence. He often plays a leadership role, but his subtle techniques mean his followers do not recognize him as a leader.

Effects of Situation-Purpose

Studies have shown that one must consider the total situation concerning "leaders" and "leadership." One factor is who the followers in a group are. Another is the purpose for which the group is formed. These contribute markedly to a leader's emergence or election. A leader in one situation may be a follower or non-participant in another.

For example, one man, accepted as a leader in his profession because of his knowledge and professional interest, has as a hobby an exceptionally fine garden. He is a competent horticulturist and belongs to a local garden club. However, he takes no active part in this club. For him, this is recreation. He does not want to assume responsibilities in this situation.

Anyone interested in leadership should realize that three basic ingredients are:

1. Those who form the group and will be the followers;
2. The conditions under which these exist;
3. The goals or purposes for which they have come to inter-relate.

94

Other important aspects are the individual motives which caused the relationship among the people involved, and what each conceives as the group's goal.

Obviously, leaders can emerge and influence their followers' activities without necessarily having personal contact. This is true of national and international leaders, and those of professional or other associations. However, the following discussion will primarily concern situations where there will be personal interaction.

Definition of Leadership

A very simple definition of leadership is "fulfilling the needs of the followers." As long as someone can fulfill and attempts to fulfill the needs of others, they will accept him as a leader. This sounds relatively simple, but we must remember that the members of the group he attempts to lead are individuals. Each has his own specific needs. If individuals band together to work toward a common goal which they all accept, and if the leader can hold them together and move them toward the goal in a way acceptable to them, that leader will be accepted. If the group changes its concept of what the goal is, or reaches the goal, they may continue to accept, *or* they may reject the leader.

Back around 1947, a class at Boston University composed mostly of World War II veterans contained several who had served under General George S. Patton. I asked whether or not they thought General Patton was a great leader.

Several students who had served under him had terrific admiration for him. They admired him because of his strict authoritarian approach, his insistence on "spit and polish," and the fact that he was physically their leader by being always "out in front." Others who had served under him frankly stated that they "hated his guts." They felt that he risked his men's lives, and was "bull-headed," primarily a showoff, interested in his own success and exploiting his men for personal glory. It is obvious that these students had quite different needs when in the service. Some saw these needs fulfilled, while others felt their needs denied.

Leadership Functions

No matter how the leader comes into his role, whether elected, appointed, born to it, or emerging, if he is to succeed in maintaining his followers and move them toward decisions and actions, he must understand certain things. These *can* be learned.

1. *He should have empathy.* Empathy is *not* sympathy. It means putting yourself in the other fellow's role, trying to understand his feelings while at the same time remaining objective. The leader must know as rapidly as possible the others of the group and try to see the frame of reference from which they operate.

2. *He must be open-minded.* He must always reexamine his personal convictions in relation to the beliefs and thinking of others. He must maintain this objectivity and refrain from value judgments.

He must realize that no situation is all black or all white, but all shades of gray. We cannot make ethical judgments or moral statements about behavior being definitely good or bad. There may be extenuating circumstances and the need to evaluate in terms of the total situation. This means considering both the present situation and its future consequences.

3. *He must appraise the social situation.* One who is going to accept a leadership role must first try to understand the social situation in which he finds himself. He should ask himself, "What am I doing here? What needs within myself am I trying to fulfill? What is my relationship with these other people? How well do they know me, and how well do I know them? What is the probable reason for their getting together? Have they set themselves a simple task, or an extremely complex one? Is it something requiring a great deal of time, or can it be easily understood?

The important thing here is to listen. Anyone who is going to lead must listen to try to learn what is going on around him. He may check his interpretation of someone's statement by asking "Do I understand that what you mean . . . ?" He then tells what he understands the other to be saying.

Anyone assuming leadership must have a good, clear grasp of the total situation in which he operates. Next, he must ask, "How well do I know these people? To what extent do I understand their basic needs? How many came because they were asked to be here? How many came because a certain amount of social pressure forced them to?" I have seen an individual sit through two 2½-hour sessions, listening, asking questions, checking, then, at the third meeting, taking over leadership in the most competent way. It is important that a person who is going to assume leadership know how each person sees the situation, and how each can contribute something to it, in a way that will satisfy him. The leader must know the potentials of individuals, their possible contribution to the task at hand.

4. *Timing* is important. You often hear someone say "I said that 10 minutes ago and nobody listened!" This is true; the group was not then ready to listen. There is no point trying to lead a group, make suggestions, or get action unless it is ready to accept the idea. It must go through several steps to get ready:

a. It must generally agree what the task is.
b. It must have some idea how to handle the task.
c. It must be ready to work on the problem.
d. The leader must help the group move along the course it has decided upon for solving the problem. At this time, it is important that he realize he should share leadership with any and all who can help hold the group together and move it toward the task's completion.

5. *Sensitivity* is another aspect of leadership. The leader must deal with any conflict within a group.

Sometimes this requires letting the people get rid of their psychological energy. This, too, is a matter of timing. In leadership, one recognizes the old saying, "A man convinced against his will, is of the same opinion still." The leader must not argue with other group members, but always remain objective. He must listen carefully to understand whether the person says what he means. Often, a person who consciously or unconsciously does not wish to be outspoken may say something which is revealing to the sensitive listener.

For example, at the third meeting of a very permissively run class, a lengthy discussion developed about an altercation between a Harvard faculty member and a police reporter, which had been reported in the morning papers. The group discussed other things, but this held their attention. They discussed it for almost an hour. Then, the group's trainer asked if they realized what they were actually talking about. After some thought and discussion, one member suddenly realized that they had been discussing the role of the authority figure and to what extent someone in authority should or could push others around.

They were actually talking about *their* group-leader-trainer. They wondered about his role, and to what extent they could push him around, actually defy him and get away with it.

The person who has trained himself to "listen with a third ear" and "to see with a third eye" has developed sensitivity. He can understand what

99

real forces operate within a group. He will know when to call the group's attention to them for the benefit of all concerned.

6. *Taking Bearings.* Another role the leader plays is to check the group periodically to see where it is. This is like checking the road map and mileage signs when driving. "Where did we start? How far have we gone? Where are we? Which way should we best go now?" The leader himself need not make such statements. He may ask someone in the group to contribute, and check this by having another evaluate the summary.

7. *Shared leadership.* Our culture heavily emphasizes the role of authority. We have to go back only a few generations to realize this, particularly in the role of the father, or in religion. We also have the authority role of the head of the company, the boss, etc.

After centuries of teaching respect and obedience to authority figures, we are beginning to question the value of the dictatorial type of authority. It is true that some individuals feel secure only in situations where all their acts are prescribed. They feel that if they obey unquestioningly, everything they do will be "all right." But most modern people resent this, and call it "regimentation."

Modern conditions require that man change to meet them. We believe that he can train and improve himself as civilization progresses. In order to encourage man to push himself intellectually, we have changed our point of view in education, science, business, and the home. We now encourage people to try to develop new and original ideas. We feel that this is not possible under strict authority and "blind obedience" alone.

This raises a new concept of leadership and the development of people. Today, the social scientist believes that *everyone* can develop some leadership qualities. We find we can accomplish a great deal more by cooperation. Therefore, we are beginning to teach people the importance of cooperation and "shared leadership". We deal more with this subject in the chapter on Decision-Making. For the moment, it is important to remember that leadership is learned and not inborn.

It is also important to realize that everyone should be able to step in and help a group move forward, by exercising leadership for some period of time. This raises a question of whether we will have "too many chiefs, and too few Indians." The importance of followership is discussed later.

Here, let us point out that someone with good leadership qualities also has the capacity for good followership.

8. *Permissiveness*. Anyone responsible for the functioning of a group, as leader, moderator, chairman, or some other role, finds himself very much in the position of a horseman. He learns to give the group its head, to learn with which capacities he must deal. This requires that while giving this freedom, he is attentive and sensitive to the response to his

permissiveness. He also knows that at any moment he may have to check the group's "headiness," exert enough control to keep behavior organized and moving forward constructively. Permissiveness implies behavior with awareness and consent of all concerned. It also implies that the permit may be revoked. It is not entirely a hands-off, *laissez-faire* attitude.

It is the duty of the supervisor, executive or any other person in the chain of command to see that the job or production is done in the most efficient way, for the benefit of all concerned. It is also important for him that he see the individuals under him are allowed to mature, grow and assume responsibility to the full extent of their potential. He should look for the greatest good for the greatest number, *not* for individual ego-enhancement.

9. *Setting standards.* Standards of behavior are needed for the good of the greatest number. All groups, even new ones, set up such standards when they begin to function. (This is sometimes unconscious.) Individuals from a certain group may bring their standards into a *new* group. Such transferred standards may or may not be acceptable.

In setting standards, it is necessary to draw attention to existing standards, and to any that outside authority may impose. There are always standards set by outside forces; no group can control all of its standards entirely. There are such natural limitations as weather and physical fitness.

And, although we may talk about "permissiveness", moving toward anarchy is not realistic. The members of all groups, particularly their leaders, must understand the standards that develop, and be able to evaluate their implications for the future. What may be adequate today may not be suitable tomorrow. Change is rapid, and may affect behavior standards.

Essential to this is the basic concept of individual human dignity, and the realization that there must be ethical standards based on individual responsibility. This responsibility is not only for the individual, but also for those with whom he is in contact.

10. *Followership*. Training in leadership also requires that we train people in the art of "followership." A good follower makes himself aware of the total situation in a group with certain problems or tasks. Like a good leader, he tries to reach a rapid understanding of the situation. Next, he determines how he can contribute. His contribution gives him satisfaction. He looks for ways in which he can be constructive to the total group.

A leader wants support from his followers. A follower can keep paying attention to what goes on around him, and support the current leader. Such support implies that he agrees with the situation. He may temporarily assume leadership by explaining the situation to others who do not understand.

The follower also lets the group know if he does not agree, or does not understand the situation.

It is also up to him to show other group members any areas where his abilities might be useful. Perhaps he can contribute experience or special skills to some aspects of the group's task.

Summary and Analysis

We have seen that leadership is skill, ability, and understanding in helping others fulfill their needs in such a way that the group being led will maintain itself, and will forward to complete its task, solve its problem, or make a decision. The individuals who can cooperate and help fulfill each other's needs in this way will form a well-integrated group.

The leader's most important role is understanding the members of the group and their needs, and having a clear concept of the task at hand and its possible outcome. He must be sure that the group's goals are *possible* and *worthwhile*.

Timing is very important—knowing *what* to say, *when* to say it, and *how* to say it most effectively.

Finally, there is the need to be able to share leadership, to adapt, to realize that other people may have contributions to make, and ways to see and do things which, viewed objectively, may be considerably better than those the original leader held.

Now, knowing this, let us evaluate the meeting called by Mr. Mullins, described earlier. Let us consider him as a leader, in terms of this chapter.

1. Mullins lacked consideration, time-wise, for the group. It would have been better had he called each staff member and asked him to the meeting. It would not have been difficult to find a convenient day and hour for only eight people. Since the memo was delivered Tuesday, Mullins probably made his plans Monday afternoon or early Tuesday morning. Notice by phone would have given the staff more planning time. If Mullins was unable to call, he could have had his secretary do so.

2. The way in which he signed the memo with his title, and the method of expression, indicate that he is a benevolent autocrat.

3. Mullins apparently did not consider the speed at which some of the items might have been handled. The first item on the agenda requires the most time! Getting simple problems out of the way first gives a feeling of accomplishment to and heartens a group. Mullins lacks sensitivity toward the group; the staff would get satisfaction from starting with simple items and making fairly rapid decisions. This would set the tempo for the meeting.

4. He stresses punctuality but is late himself! This adds to the group's frustration. Had he planned carefully, he would not have been late. If he had found it impossible to be on time, he should have sent a message asking the staff to start the meeting and make decisions on the simpler items to be covered. A well-integrated group should be able to assume responsibilities and begin to

make decisions. Obviously, he and his staff lacked confidence in each other.

5. His breezy manner and method of opening the meeting is a threat or "dare" to the group. It increases the frustration already caused by the memo, his poor timing and his tardiness.

6. Exercising the leadership role of the benevolent autocrat, he takes up much time expressing *his* ideas and feelings.

7. After assuming the definite benevolent autocratic role, and one of "omnipotent personality", he then tosses the whole thing to his staff by saying he lacks pertinent information and hopes some of them can give it to him. A leader such as Jack Mullins is very apt to find a certain amount of passive resistance from members of his staff. He will be completely unable to understand this, since, in his own opinion, he is a "good fellow" and really wants his staff to be democratic—he thinks.

8. Mullins did not appraise the social situation when he arrived, but plunged right into his own ideas.

9. Certainly his timing was off in regard to his memo, his lateness, and his handling of the material.

10. He is quite obviously not in the habit of sharing leadership with his staff. He has no intention of doing so, as he immediately assumed a dominant role.

11. His blasé attitude all through the memo and in his comments shows a complete lack of sensitivity to the feelings of the members of his staff.

12. He is not interested in other people's opinions, nor does he concern himself with the group's present position. Ideally, the group should have begun by talking about the agenda in a relatively informal fashion, and formulated tentative conclusions, but the door had already been closed to this.

They have no doubt been talking among themselves about some of the items. It would be well if Mullins opened the discussion by asking if they had discussed the agenda, and what ideas they had about it. From even an informal discussion, they may have reached an informal decision or general opinion on what should be done about a couple of the items. These could have been dealt with very rapidly, were Mullins a competent leader.

In fact, if Mullins had taken a cup of coffee himself on arriving, and had listened, he could have sized up the atmosphere and known to what extent the staff was frustrated and what its general mood was. Then, had he been able to feel with the group, he would have known what sort of opening comment would establish a good relation with it. Perhaps members could have worked off their frustrations and gone on to the business at hand.

There is no doubt that members of Mullins' staff have some friendship and warmth towards him, due to his attempts to be a good fellow. On the other hand, their feelings must be ambivalent, since he also annoys them. They probably have some conflict in their own minds concerning their attitudes toward him.

Mullins has failed his group. His staff can see no way

in which he is attempting to help them in their own personal growth toward assuming responsibility and living up to their individual potentials.

This commonplace situation points up the fact that good intentions are no substitute for adequate training in leadership. Mullins' errors were all preventable. His mistakes were costly, certainly in terms of staff morale and undoubtedly also in dollars and cents.

CHAPTER EIGHT

Decision-Making

Case Study of a Poor Decision

Don Matthews, plant manager of the Bontex Manufacturing Company, sat at the head of the board table in the conference room.

"Well," he said, looking around the table, "I guess we've discussed this enough. You all know my opinion. I think the only way to bring this to a satisfactory conclusion now is to vote on it, and I think you will agree with me on this point. Let me summarize the point of view, then one of you can make a motion.

"With the opening of the new parking space next week, all employees will have to park there. Furthermore, no employees are to park along the plant on Walnut Street. This area will be left open for visitors, salesmen coming here, and members of employees' families picking them up when the worker doesn't drive to the plant. Who will make this motion? Thank you, Jack. Now, who will second it? Thank you, Tim. Now, all those in favor please raise the right hand. All right, it's a vote.

"Bill, what's the matter? You didn't vote for this. I'm surprised you didn't want to go along with the rest of the crowd. Are you still pessimistic about the whole thing? You think we may have trouble with some of the people? I'm sure we won't. They all signed the statement that they'd obey the rules of the company, and the rules now include this one about parking."

Two months later, Fred Lewis, union steward and lathe operator with a five-year unblemished record of company service, left his car all day on Walnut Street. The second day, he parked there just as the plant superintendent was going in.

"Hey, Fred," called out the superintendent, "you aren't supposed to park there. You'd better move your car."

"Says who?" Fred replied, "This is a public street, you know."

"You know the rules," said the superintendent. "You signed the agreement. I don't want any trouble but if you don't have that car moved by noon, you'll be fired." With that, the superintendent went to his office.

In the meantime, two other employees walked along with Fred.

"How about it, Fred," asked one, "are you going to move it?"

"The Hell I am," replied Fred. "This is a public street. I checked at City Hall. They can't ban us from parking here unless they get the city's O.K.—which they haven't even asked for. It's just like that bunch in the front office. They're always telling us what to do, what not to do, and never considering our feelings. If they'd asked us if we'd be *willing* to park somewhere else, I'd have agreed, I wouldn't have given it a thought. They didn't ask. They told us, and I'm going to make an issue of it."

Fred was fired. There was a grievance proceeding, at which Fred was reinstated. The city reprimanded the company for trying to usurp public authority in its company parking regulations. This led to much unfavorable publicity during the hearings, and added to the citizens' resentment toward the company.

Had Bill's objections to the parking plan been heard, this unhappy situation might never have arisen. The meeting was conducted in an undemocratic manner. In reaching a decision, the plant manager completely failed not only to listen to his subordinates, but also to know how far he was committing himself and the company. The long-range effects of this ill-attained decision were extremely injurious to the Bontex Manufacturing Company.

Decision-Making Always Involves Change

Nothing in life is constant. There is continual change. The people who work and relate with one another and who, to some extent, control the destinies of themselves and others, must always be prepared for change. In order to prepare for and to control changes, it is necessary to make decisions about future behavior.

Toward the end of World War II, the New England Confectionery Company realized that, as new machinery became available, a number of changes in the plant would be necessary. Management was concerned as to how these changes might best be made. It desired very much to enlist employee cooperation, in order to avoid the usual resistance. They obtained the services of F. Alexander Magoun of Human Relations, Inc. as a consultant.

At the company's annual Christmas party, a play written by Magoun, "Joe Necco Comes Home," was presented. The plot concerned the changes that the Necco family wanted to make to improve their house in anticipation of their son's return from military service. Employees seeing the play soon sensed the message that changes were about to occur in the "Necco" plant.

The next step was to organize the election of representatives within the various departments who could communicate information to workers, and channel responses back to management. The company successfully alerted its employees to coming changes; their acceptance of such changes was extremely gratifying.

Implementing Decision-Making for Change

When a group must make a decision, such a decision is never an isolated act. If a father forbids his teen-age son to use the car, he also may be providing such alternatives as:

The son's girl breaking the date because she won't ride the bus;

Mother slipping Junior five dollars for a taxi;

Son riding with a classmate who is an irresponsible driver;

Son taking the car without permission—and so on through any number of possible alternatives.

Decision-making involves not only one issue, but probably a main issue and a number of subsidiary problems. In the case cited at the beginning of this chapter, the primary problem was parking facilities for salesmen and visitors. A secondary problem was facilities for employees' families to "live park" to pick up workers. Issues not even considered included informing workers of the new rule, how to enlist their cooperation, whether such a ruling should be in the labor contract, or whether the previously-signed statement of obedience would cover parking rules. Further issues included what penalties would be enforced if the regulation was broken, and the extent to which the company regulation might conflict with city ordinances.

FIRST STEP

Before issues can be decided, or a decision made, however, a "socializing" process must go on. No matter how well members of a group may know each other, there is always a preliminary interval during which one inquires about the individual's health, his family, the weather, or the day's news. If the members of the group are well acquainted, such preliminaries are brief. In no case may they be omitted entirely in favor of a gruff "Let's get down to business" approach.

These preliminaries give people a chance to "feel out" the moods of others. Is someone angry, worried, preoccupied, or unusually talkative? Such moods may govern his behavior, and must be taken into account by those dealing with him. This socializing is therefore the first step in decision-making. (In case the reader thinks that this step can be omitted where decision-making is solitary, the obvious retort is that *no* decision-making involves just one person.)

SECOND STEP

The second step of the decision-making process is learning the *real issue*. Often, this is flatly stated by a person who assumes leadership of the group, as in the case at the beginning of the chapter. If the determination of the issue is opened to general discussion, a number of related issues are settled. In the parking situation, such a "minor issue" was the question of whether the company had a right to make regulations about the use of a public thoroughfare. The first step might have been to learn what the city ordinances said regarding parking. Too often, decisions are made on what seem to be the paramount issues, without a complete exploration of the related or even preliminary issues which must be decided upon first.

If one stands slightly to the right of a mirror and looks at the image, he will get a somewhat different view of his background and surroundings than if he moves to the center of the mirror, or to the extreme left. "How it looks," we say, "depends on where you stand." To obtain as complete a picture of a problem as possible one must try to view it from every angle. In decision-making, the individual comments of all members of the group give perspective. The total situation is more likely to be seen when we look through several pairs of eyes, rather than just one pair.

The competent leader of a decision-making group

summarizes and clarifies the issues expressed. He gets feedback from the group. If the group consists of people who know each other, have worked together, and have a common interest in getting the job done well, the determination of the issue or issues does not take long. But if the individuals in the group are not acquainted, or seem to be resentful of some of the statements made, no effective decision-making can occur. If there seems to be blocking, and no "meeting of minds" the good group leader will try to diagnose the obstruction to progress. The issues may need more clarification. Or, one or more group members may have some "hidden agenda" (a personal bias, opinion, or prejudice) which prevents him from seeing the problem as a whole.

The best decision-making is by groups trained in the steps of decision-making, where all are acquainted and have mutual respect. Such a group rapidly creates a permissive atmosphere where each feels he can speak frankly. In such groups, frankness often receives criticism, but the criticism is of the ideas, *not* the person. Where individuals are among strangers, or where they feel in jeopardy if they express themselves frankly, the hidden agendas make trouble.

An excellent film produced by the National Training Laboratory is called "Hidden Committees". It depicts a group of townspeople representing various interests, brought together to discuss juvenile delinquency. Each member of the group has a committee sitting behind him, symbolizing the people who influence his life. The union member has his wife as an influence. She is very concerned about the problem of juvenile delinquency, because their son has been involved in an escapade in which he was seriously hurt. She therefore pleads with her husband to take firm steps for community action.

But also behind her husband is a union representative. He points out that he must not take any forceful stand, as this may reflect upon the union, which is currently anxious to avoid being conspicuous in the community. Thus, the union member, caught between these two forces, cannot cooperate with the rest of the group. But if the union member is in a group where he feels respect and trust, he can openly express these diametrically opposed points of view. Then, the rest of the group is able to discuss them with him; he is helped to reach a decision without feelings of guilt or pressure.

THIRD STEP

The third step in the decision-making process is for the group to decide how it will reach a decision. The group may agree to let each person speak in turn. It may decide to list all the suggestions and to discuss each for a limited time, as it is offered. Or, they may gather ideas into a list, and then discuss and evaluate the suggestions, one by one. The method is less important than advance agreement on a method. Unfortunately, each of us is apt to become "ego-involved", and to feel that our opinion is the only one. We are especially prone to persist in an opinion if we have the support of one or two others. We come into opposition with another who holds a different, and equally supported opinion, and a prolonged argument ensues. Very often, those involved in such an argument fail to listen to the others.

We have all heard two people arguing, when it is apparent that basically they are in agreement. Each has failed to understand the other. We have already referred to this problem in the chapter on communication. Some groups contain a "peace-maker" who is skilled at tactfully showing the common thread of agreement among dissenters. A genuine dissenter should always be given the opportunity to express his point of view fully. Bill, in the parking situation, was such a dissenter. Minority opinion is worth listening to and summarizing to see if it has value, or may alter majority opinion.

The author has seen a committee of seven people try to make a decision and finally arrive at a six-to-one vote. Being trained in decision-making, the six sat back and asked the non-conformist why he disagreed. After his explanation, the six agreed that he was right—and all changed their votes!

A person can often be forced to agree with his peers through psychological pressure, or to agree with his superior by the implicit threat of authority. But "a man convinced against his will is of the same opinion still". Such a man is not really committed to the decision the group has made. Fred, in the parking case, was such a man. His resistance to group decision stirred up a lot of trouble.

FOURTH STEP

The fourth step of decision-making is evaluation of trial decisions. A check must be made on progress. Trial solutions must be tested. Often, things will arise which will affect the decisions, so that the group's point of view will change. We are sometimes very fearful of trying to produce change, feeling that the need for new experience and the need for security which were described in Chapter 4 somehow conflict with each other. There is actually no conflict. Change often maintains security, because "keeping up to date" is more satisfying than being "old-fashioned" or "behind the times."

Let us suppose that we seek security through maintaining the affectionate, closely-knit aspect of family life. If we require our adult children to keep a ten o'clock curfew, we alienate them, and jeopardize the familial security. If, however, we "move with the times" and give our children a house key and a later curfew, these concessions to the modern way of life ensure the family affection and stability. In the same way, in business and industrial life the individual accepts change if those who influence his destiny are people in whom he has confidence. His security is not threatened by change if he continues to know what is expected of him in the organization, and that these expectations are reasonable.

Getting Decisions Accepted

Change *can* be threatening in such situations as that of the Bontex Manufacturing Company. It is acceptable in such a situation as that of the New England Confectionery Company. Where the people involved have real hand in decision-making involving change, they respond enthusiastically, because the participants themselves have discovered the need for it and wish to bring it about.

The tentative solutions involved in decision-making are an example of the shared leadership we discussed in Chapter Seven. Through such sharing, it is possible for each member of the group to see not only all the "angles" of a situation, but the interrelated whole, in terms of the entire context of the organization involved. Under these circumstances, the individuals dealing with the problem are personally motivated and involved. They are willing to try to foresee the long-range results of their decisions, and to take on personal commitments in order to bring about change based on their decisions. This actual decision-making, with a full facing of the responsibilities involved, is the fifth step of the decision-making process. The individual participants have put selfish considerations aside. They have thought and acted in terms of each other's welfare and the good of their organization.

Quite different, alas, was the decision-making at the Bontex Manufacturing Company. Had this company gone through the steps just discussed, the plant superintendent would have sent out a notice suggesting that something should be done about the parking situation. When the department heads met, he should not have expressed his own opinions, but should have learned what the others thought of the problem. Bill would have presented his objections, which might have included the point of view later expressed by Fred, who defied the edict. The city ordinances would have been studied, thus avoiding the embarrassment of a company regulating public highway parking. Tentative solutions would have been discussed without animosity. Objections would have had respectful attention. Finally, a group decision would have been reached and adequately communicated to all members of the organization so that their cooperation and support would have been forthcoming. Had such steps of decision-making been carried out, an unpleasant and faulty decision would have been avoided.

True, it is easy to be wise *after* the event! How can such errors in decision-making be *avoided?* The obvious answer is that in order for groups to work together in a constructive way, they must have some experience in this area. This means that they need training, and that is the subject of the next chapter.

CHAPTER NINE

Human Relations Training

John Lampson, president of the Riverdale Manufacturing Company, looked across the luncheon table at Paul Newhall, head of the personnel department.

"Paul," he said, "there may be something to this human relations jazz we've been hearing about. I'm convinced that our company has to get on the ball, and be modernized in various ways. I've called in a group of engineers who are working on some new ideas, but I'm concerned about the employees. I gather that some of the big firms now referring to their human relations departments mean something over and beyond personnel. Apparently it goes into industrial and community relations.

"You've had some experience in the area. I'd appreciate it if you could come up with some suggestions as to how we might go about this. I think the company is in good enough shape so that we can spend a reasonable amount of money on the project. If we have to, I think we could bring in some experts to help us out. I'd appreciate it very much if you'd prepare a general report of what it's all about. Then we can go over it and perhaps lay out a specific program."

A week later, a memorandum entitled "A General Program for Human Relations Training for the Riverdale Manufacturing Company" was on Mr. Lampson's desk. It read as follows:

Objectives

The objective of a training program in human relations is to help the members of the entire organization reach a better understanding of themselves and their relationships with other members of the company. Specifically, such a program will help people to gain insights into themselves and those with whom they come in contact, not only at their own level in the organization, but also with those with whom they inter-relate, to whom they are responsible, and whom they are responsible for, whether they are above, below, or in the same level of the organization.

It is anticipated that such a program will result in people who are more satisfied to belong to our organization. As a result, we should have higher morale. This, in turn, will give us greater productivity and greater individual satisfaction and happiness than we have previously experienced.

To bring about such changes, we must interest each and every member of the organization, not only on behalf of himself but for the total organization. This will require each individual to re-assess his goals, and perhaps to set new ones. This will be true not only for individuals but also for each department, segment, or level of the organization. This can be brought about only when each individual is encouraged to speak frankly, critically, and constructively about himself, his role, and the total company.

Procedure

It is recommended that the program be planned at four levels of supervision: top management, middle management, lower supervisors, and production workers. The program should be instituted or begun in the above order. As soon as one program is well under way, the next one can be started. A qualified staff should be brought in to prepare the program.

METHODOLOGY

It is essential that those undergoing the training actively participate in it. Lectures and collateral reading should be held to a minimum. Some of the techniques which will be used are as follows:

1. **The incident method.** A modification of the case method.

2. **Role-playing.** A form of acting out real or imaginary situations. This is useful for individual

practice of some form of communication or act that is to be taken. Trying it out beforehand shows the individual what will result from his intended approach. He sometimes tries several approaches to a situation, to learn which is most fruitful. Another way of using role-playing is when two people disagree on a situation. They exchange roles. Each plays the other in an effort to see things from the other's point of view.

3. **Buzz groups.** People are grouped in small groups of three to six persons. Each of the buzz groups (so named because they usually consult in a large room and speak quietly so as not to bother other groups) develops its ideas, which a spokesman later communicates to all other groups. This saves time in getting large numbers of people to participate when the size of the total group is unwieldy.

4. **"Games"** are simulated situations dealing with a larger number of variables than in role-playing. The simulated situation is used to train people in certain types of decision-making, where one wishes to show the need for understanding the functions or responsibilities of various departments as they all contribute necessary knowledge for sound decisions within an organization.

5. **Creative imagination.** Sometimes called "brainstorming", this is a technique for encouraging the expression of new ideas, and stimulating people to develop completely fresh and constructive ways of solving problems.

6. **The syndicate method.** Several people prepare a report outside the work setting, on a subject which is to be dealt with by a group within the organization. This method trains people to work together, and is also an economical way, time-wise, of investigating a specific field or problem.

7. **The consultation group.** A team of three trained interviewers tackles a real problem. One uses the direct method, and makes suggestions and proffers advice to the individual with a problem. The second uses the non-directive technique and encourages the individual to find his own solutions. The third acts as observer and records the interactions. The method demonstrates that the individual possesses the resources for solving his own problems.

We can anticipate that Paul Newhall's recommendations for a human relations training program will arouse Mr. Lampson's interest and curiosity. He will want more information, in the same way that you, the reader, set about expanding the information presented in the memorandum to the president of Riverdale Manufacturing Company.

Learning

The program advocated is a *training* program, intended to bring about learning to develop skill in a particular area or capacity. Learning is the psychological term for the modification of behavior. When the infant, in his creeping about a room, touches a hot coffee pot, withdraws his hand, cries, and subsequently avoids the coffee pot, we say he has "learned" the meaning of the hot coffee pot. The infant's learning was of a simple, reflex sort. Nature had prepared his nervous system to protect him in this way. Touching an object which produced pain resulted in an immediate withdrawal from the pain-producing object. Here we had a learning experience where a specific stimulation produced a modification of behavior (i.e. avoidance or not-touching).

Not all learning is so simple. When the baby who learned about the hot coffee pot reaches school-age, he must have learned to hold back his wetting until it is time to go to the toilet; to wait until the traffic policeman signals before crossing the street to go to school; to sit quietly in his chair in the classroom while the teacher explains the difference between the letters "d" and "b". By the time he is in junior high school, the same child will be memorizing poems, and the names and political parties of the presidents of the United States. He will be using mathematical concepts in arithmetic and algebra. Perhaps he will be a member of the class council and hold office. In any event, he will vote for the class officers.

All these, and many more things, constitute his daily learning experiences. His learning has become infinitely more complex. When he was a baby, his response to the hot coffee pot was immediate, and in his own interest. Withdrawal protected him. As a teen-ager, he cannot always see "what good" for him lies in remembering historical events, manipulating mathematical symbols, or joining his classmates in the class regulatory activities. Since the ultimate goal of such learning cannot always be understood, the teachers try to motivate him by relating his new learning experience to previous learning, and by building into the learning process immediate gratifications.

To produce such results, the teacher uses a variety of techniques. An economics class can be made interested in the stock market by collectively owning a single share of stock. The mathematics class can concern itself with the area of shade cast by the school building, and its effect upon the kind of plants which may be used for decorating the school grounds. Before-and-after motion pictures can demonstrate the validity of slum clearance better than a hundred impassioned editorials. The job of the trainer or the educator is to understand his objectives, then seek ways to implement his purposes which will carry appeal for the student.

Human relations training aspires to teaching the individual to modify his behavior so that he becomes more effective in relating to other human beings, especially in the work situation. In order to understand others, the individual must start by improving his self-understanding. He must develop a high degree of objectivity, approaching problems of human relations as if they were outside himself. In this way, he can identify the actual problem, collect information, make a judgment, and check that judgment. Said otherwise, human relations training applies the scientific method to the interrelationships of people. In order to collect information accurately, the human relations trained individual must be sensitive to the feelings and attitudes of others.

It has already been pointed out that in making and implementing judgments (decision-making), the individual must understand he is making certain commitments for the future. The individual who is "human relations trained" has learned to become a "good group member" and to develop his ability to assume leadership functions. His leadership is not a matter of "bossing," but of encouraging others to participate in attaining the group's objectives.

Under these circumstances, it is pointless to undertake any program of human relations training for workers unless the "top echelon" is solidly behind such a program. Mr. Lampson's keen interest is an encouraging factor in the program proposed for the Riverdale Manufacturing Company. All writers in the area of human relations training agree that real success comes only for the program in which *top management* itself *is involved*. In addition to strong endorsement and participation in the training program, it is important for management to have a complete understanding of the organization, how it was formed, what its purpose is, and the roles of individuals in it. Such information must be available to all members of the organization, as has been pointed out already in an earlier chapter.

Human relations training should bring about personality growth. This should increase individuals' ability to communicate with each other and to participate in shared leadership, in order to produce constructive change through good decision-making.

LEARNING BY DOING

In the classroom and in industry alike, the phrase "learning by doing" is appropriate. Being ordered to change, or directed to learn, will not necessarily cause modification of behavior. One can read a driver's manual and remain unable to operate an automobile, or see a film on first-aid but lack ability to deal with an injured person. There is need for a direct experience, and what we call ego-involvement. Human relations training tries, therefore, to create situations in which the individual behaves spontaneously, and in which his experiences make him wish to *change* his behavior.

An illustration is role-playing. In a university class where interviewing was being taught, a class member who was employed in business discussed an ordeal which lay ahead of him—discharging a woman employee the following day. He was invited to act out the dismissal with a girl member of the class, while the group observed. He "spoke his piece" in a "stuffy" manner, with some embarrassment. The girl who had played the part of the employee being dismissed frankly revealed her feelings about the experience. Other girls in the class gave him further insights. He experimented with different ways of handling the situation, with other people taking the role of the individual to be discharged. At the next class meeting, he reported, with some elation, that his mission had been accomplished. The employee had thanked him for separating her from a job in which she was actually unhappy! This success was due not to rehearsing particular techniques, but from his insight into feminine psychology, and basic human needs, which he had utilized in his actual separation interview. This is "learning by doing."

The Importance of the Trainer

Human relations training must be carried out by a qualified trainer, leader, or teacher. Such a person sets up specific goals and encourages the trainees to move toward those goals, which are new modes of feeling and behaving. The trainer must be aware of the individual differences in personality of those whom he is training. He must be sensitive to the feelings and needs of others. For example, he does not select the shyest person in the group to role-play before the entire group at its first meeting! Nor does he set forth a role-playing situation for a first attempt which is "loaded with dynamite." Rather, he defines a situation which will minimize embarrassment and give the participants feelings of accomplishment. Timing of training exercises, and the choice of appropriate ones, is an important responsibility of a trainer. He must be extremely versatile in the training techniques and resources at his command.

Keep in mind that the training techniques presented to the reader are only for background and understanding, not for his use! A novice who uses role-playing or the incident method will have more on his hands than he bargained for, and will do irremediable harm! It is always interesting, and appalling, to see that people who would not dream of practicing medicine because they lack medical training may not hesitate to utilize psychological methods which also require professional training and experience! An expert human relations consultant is ordinarily required for initiating a human relations training program.

The reader may demur at this point, and think of persons whom he knows who have an extraordinary ability to relate well with other people, who show sensitivity, and who experience a need to modify their own behavior in order to help others to greater accomplishment. There are such people, and they often do a marvelous job, but they are not aware of the reasons for their success. Thus, they cannot pass on to others their special insights, and skills. They are good practitioners, but not always good teachers.

We know this from daily life. Many a man can "tinker" with an automobile engine and restore it to its former efficiency, but he could not conduct a course in automobile repair. He may lack the talent for communicating with others in the field of his competency. Some of the people with sensitivity and social skills will profit by training, and eventually may become trainers themselves. There are also some persons who have the potential to develop good human relations ability but need training in developing insight and acquiring skills. They, too, respond to training and can become productive and helpful in a well established human relations program. A third group is composed of people with rather rigid personality structures. Such individuals have developed serviceable techniques by "trial and error" which work for them in routine situations.

A first-line supervisor may get on extremely well with his men because he leaves them pretty much alone. In an emergency situation, such an individual may become quite emotional and autocratic; his men will not "go along with him." This type of individual can be helped to get on better with others, but he will probably never be able to take over human relations training responsibilities. Thus, it is desirable for human relations training to be instituted by an outside specialist, who trains selected individuals to carry on subsequent training after the program is well under way and the specialist himself has departed.

Motivation

Everything that was written in Chapter Four is applicable to training procedures. Human relations training must relate to the needs of the organization's members. The young man who had the responsibility of dismissing a subordinate had a strong need for belonging and acceptance. He felt uncomfortable about being disliked by a discharged employee. He wanted to perform his task competently, because he had a strong need for recognition. With this strong internal motivation, he was very responsive to the points of view advanced by the young women in the class. He profited by what they had explained to him, because of his strong motivation. Had he been a pig-headed, opinionated young egotist, he could not have been helped, because motivation would have been lacking.

Most people respond to a human relations training program, provided they do not believe it to be a "gimmick" or a means of "brain-washing" them. Human beings, as we have stated, are "social animals." They want to get on with other human beings, to be liked, respected, and trusted. Unfortunately, some of them have built up bad habits, from poor teaching earlier in life. Such people are often defensive. They ridicule the courtesy approach to others which say, "ask, don't order." They ask, derisively, "What kind of an army would we have if the general had to say to a private, 'Buddy, would you mind policing the parade ground?' "

Yet, today, where even the military has tempered its authoritativeness, such individuals find the "tough approach" unrewarding in business and industry. A skilled human relations trainer often motivates these individuals by letting them try their methods in the group situation. He encourages the group to do its own disciplining of its members. When the authoritarian person comes up against the psychological barrier of group resistance, he often develops insight, and responds to human relations training.

In the "resistant" category we also find the person with the attitude of "Go ahead and try it, but I know it won't work." His attitude is a step towards progress, because he is exposing himself to training. Psychologists refer to the "Law of Readiness" or the condition of being motivated to learn. When an individual is ready, he can be taught. Another psychological law which has application to human relations training is the "Law of Use" which states that the more frequently a behavior is undertaken, the greater the likelihood of its persistence.

VARIETY OF STIMULATION

In writing about communication, we pointed out that the wider the evocation of sensory images, the greater the likelihood of communication. In human relations training, the lecture method is used but not emphasized. Every attempt is made to present material in a variety of ways. Motion pictures, taped recordings of group discussions, role-playing and incident method, reports, charts, diagrams and other pictorial methods are used. Cases, for example, may be presented by the media of film strip and recordings and/or by motion pictures, and/or by situations written up in detail, and/or role-playing in which people act out the situation being discussed.

After trainees receive information, they may respond to it by writing or delivering a report, or working with other members of their group in a discussion which is taped, or by role-playing aspects of the situation.

An especially interesting training technique is that of Paul Pigors, of the Massachusetts Institute of Technology. He gives his trainees the "bare bones" of a situation, which he calls an "incident" or occurrence. It is actually a real-life situation. The trainees must collect the essential data in order to make decisions about the situation. The trainer is a resource person and has full data on the "incident," but he only yields the items to the person who requests the information. This type of training tends to sharpen the perceptive abilities of the trainees. They learn to look for essentials, rather than opinions or irrelevant data.

Role-playing, to which several references have already been made, can be a very important human relations training method. The individuals acting in such situation are asked to operate from another person's frame of reference. Each individual is privately supplied with information about the person whose role he is to act. He tries to "feel and think himself into the part", and to behave as he imagines the person whose role he is playing would behave. Sometimes a person is put into a role directly contrary to his usual one. Thus, in a telephone company an operator role-played her supervisor and the supervisor role-played her subordinate. Each learned from the experience. Role reversals are used only after the trainees have had experience in playing "straight roles" with which they can comfortably identify. For example, a man is not ordinarily asked to play a feminine role as his acting would be a mere caricature of his notion of feminine mannerisms. People can only play roles which bear some relationship to their real personalities. Thus, role-playing does *not* require acting ability, as so many people suppose.

Sometimes, in role-playing before a training group, someone takes exception to the way a role is handled. He may be asked to step in and take over the role. He may then find himself in the same difficulties as the original role player. Or, if he is able to play the role more suitably, his amended version can be a lesson for the individual who "stepped out" of the role. It is obvious that situations like this can be fraught with emotional tension—another reason why such techniques should be used only by the experienced trainer or teacher.

Case studies are useful in human relations training, especially when the materials come from the company's own experience. This helps trainees to see how to prepare to cope with the type of problems they will meet.

Specific Company Benefits

In addition to the general benefits of human relations training which already have been cited, a program often yields specific benefits which had not been anticipated when it was inaugurated. Careful observation and record-keeping during the training program helps management to recognize potentials for growth among employees of all levels. Individuals are often discovered who are doing a fine job in their present placement, but who have qualities which would enable them to do a superb job in another position.

Since Western Electric's Hawthorne Plant experiments, there has been a growing belief that first-line supervisors should be equipped and trained to do some counseling with the people under them. This is a change from the idea that the first-line foreman should be a "real sergeant" extremely authoritative, and preoccupied with "getting the work out." Today's first-line foreman, who is skilled in human relations, has a deep interest in and appreciation of the people in his department. He can not only "get the work out," but have his workers enjoy the process. His workers will discuss not only work, but personal problems with such a man.

This is in no way a suggestion that the foreman should become a psychotherapist. Rather, we are saying that such a foreman can be trained to act as a responsible leader. When something is beyond his capacity he knows the proper channels through which to route the problem. Such a responsibility erases from this job the label of "the forgotten man." Instead of being "caught" between management and the worker, he can act as liaison to make smoother operation of the organization possible.

Human relations training should operate from the top down, and embrace every member of the organization. The purpose is to help every individual to develop his innate capacity for understanding himself and others, and helping others to understand themselves. The basic essentials are the abilities to listen, to empathize, to reflect, and to create situations in which two-way communication is free and frank. It is thus possible for individuals to know each other and feel mutual respect for their particular abilities. An understanding of the needs of superiors, subordinates, and peers promotes feelings of well-being throughout the organization. If the top-to-bottom coverage has been used in the training program, every aspect of the operation should benefit. Not the least of such benefits is the improved satisfaction of company personnel, which leads to increased zest and efficiency on the job.

CHAPTER TEN

The Manager and Human Relations

The Influence of Technology

Our way of life has altered tremendously in a generation or two. The "little red schoolhouse" has given way to a complicated modern installation with public address system, platoon classes, and automated language "labs." A bicycle repairman's small shop has developed into a gigantic automobile service complex. Two decades have seen "science-fiction" become reality. In general, two directions of change seem to be especially influential in altering our lives. One is the rapid development of automation, the other, utilization of new sources of energy. Already, we feel personal pressures from these two influences. Most of us have shivered when we think of an "electric eye" scrutinizing our federal income tax return in the future! With awe, we hear news reports of international television broadcast relays via an orbital station. These profound changes emphasize the responsibility which those in planning situations have to be constantly prepared for change.

All those technical changes have come from the actions of human beings. People develop new inventions and new ideas which cause changes in their inter-relationships. Thus, in any progressive business, it is the job of those in leadership positions to look to the future and plan. Old concepts of organization must alter. "Bandwagon thinking" is obsolete. Instead of being committed to preserving the *status quo*, today's managers must be able to look into the future and see how it can be soundly planned for on the basis of the past.

The speedy change which characterizes today's world is developing a new type of executive. He comes into power not from wealth, birth, or family prestige, but because he has been trained in the new ways of thinking. Some writers have even gone so far as to say that today's manager must be a "general specialist." This implies that the successful contemporary executive must have considerable technical knowledge in a number of fields, and be able to integrate this knowledge. He then becomes a specialist in coordination. In order to coordinate the vast complex of a modern industry, the executive must be able to count on information and advice from others. Top management is too big a job for one man. At every management level, this same principle of consultation and cooperation is necessary. Only through other human beings can we achieve our goals.

F. Alexander Magoun, formerly a professor at Massachusetts Institute of Technology, and now a management consultant, has written in his book *Cooperation and Conflict in Industry:*

"Actually, the hope of the future is cooperation, with everyone giving his best effort on his most appropriate level, under self-respecting relationship, and without subserviency." [1]

Need for Self-Evaluation

It is essential, then, that today's manager continually study himself and others. He must plan alternative actions so that if one attack on a problem is not fruitful, he has other methods available. He must learn to recognize the danger signals in the relationships among workers; such as rumors, emotional outbursts, and horseplay, and be able to diagnose the reasons for these signals and to take appropriate action. Today's successful executive learns to operate well and to cooperate with other people. He surrounds himself with people who will give him the necessary support for the success of the enterprise and the organization.

In emphasizing the desirability of building maximum cooperativeness with one's associates, it is important to inject a word of warning. The *paramount* emotional link between the manager and his personnel should be the tie with the organization, not personal friendship. Really close friendship between the professional person and a client, patient, or student can impede an effective professional relationship. The physician, lawyer, and teacher usually know the need to maintain an "invisible

[1] *Cooperation and Conflict in Industry,* Harper's, 1960.

barrier" between themselves and the members of the public with whom they work.

Friendship is possible, but it should lie outside the professional relationship. In the same way, in business it behooves the manager to keep the interests of the organization first in dealing with company personnel, including those who may be friends. Thus, in conference, the manager might say, "Jack, how would that effect your department?" rather than, "How does it look to you, Jack?" The many interrelationships and communications with others should be in terms of common interest in the organization—emphasizing the philosophy "for the good of the company"—rather than "for the good of an individual." By focusing the goals on company interests, not personal objectives, the manager facilitates permissiveness for decision-making.

This ensures that such decision-making concerns the welfare of everyone in the organization. It minimizes the chance for others to "get at him" through emotional ties. By the same token, it protects his subordinates and associates from his exploitation.

Key management men must keep abreast of human relations literature, especially when their organizations are developing new programs. There is an enormous amount of practical study and experimentation now going on in the human relations field. The experiences of other organizations will be useful, along with reports of experimental studies at universities and workshops.

Such knowledge, coupled with a thorough understanding of one's company or organization, makes it possible to continue to develop good human relations, and modify one's techniques to meet the immediate needs of changing situations.

More than anything else, this requires creativity on the executive's part. Each manager must look to his own growth and the development of those for whom he is responsible. Management's point of view must be to *use* good human relations, *encourage others to use them*, and "let the people know." By this is meant informing not only the people within the company, but also those in the local community, of the company's philosophy and goals.

How Human Relations Pays

It is important that the company create a favorable image in the minds of those who have contact with it. This image depends very heavily on the reputation the company has concerning its treatment of workers. It can reduce recruitment problems, and encourage applicants with good potential to join an organization where they have a chance to grow.

With the rapid changes which are taking place today, it is essential that *every* member of the organization be encouraged to make his maximum contribution, whether in terms of human relations or technical skill. This presupposes the good communication system within the organization which has already been advocated in these pages. Such communications channels encourage new ideas and suggestions. Forward-looking executives are developed under a program which develops talent, promotes individuals, and eventually furnishes replacements for those who retire. This long-range point of view is the hallmark of today's good manager.

It is believed that the manager of the future will view human relations as a study of organizational behavior, and will utilize the research in the social sciences to avoid serious errors in the managing of people. Emphasis will be on understanding, rather than manipulation. Through the decentralization of decision-making which allows all members of the organization to have a part in planning the future, people develop faith in the organization. This enhances their confidence in themselves, and leads to the highest degree of cooperation in a democratic and free society.

In summary, human relations is interested in the individual as such, and in the interrelationships of individuals as they organize. In this work, therefore, we began by considering organizational structure, and the problem of morale within the group. This led us to examine ways of measuring attitudes and assessing motivation. To understand something of differing motivations, we dealt with the needs common to human beings, and showed the different ways in which some people fulfilled these needs. We described the importance of good communications in understanding needs and giving information and instructions which might help fulfill them. We emphasized the value of participation for all, and called it "shared leadership."

Such leadership, it was pointed out, gives each individual a chance for self-expression and growth. Emphasis was put on the rapid changes of today's society, and

the need for managers and employees to be psychologically and technically ready for it. To bring about
this improved state of affairs, we discussed something of
the manager's role, and his need to be informed in the
human relations area.

Finally, we pointed out that part of the preparation
for change means recognizing, training, and upgrading
new managers. It is hoped that those who read this
book will be encouraged to study and become more
active in the whole realm of human relations.

Bibliography

Argyris, Chris, *Understanding Organizational Behavior,* Dorsey Press, 1960, 179 pp.

Davis, Keith, *Human Relations at Work,* 2nd ed. McGraw-Hill, 1962, 642 pp.

Fleishman, Edwin A., *Studies in Personnel and Industrial Psychology,* Dorsey Press, 1961, 633 pp.

Hacon, R. J., *Management Training, Aims and Methods,* The English Universities Press, 102 Newgate St., London, 1961, 253 pp.

Heckman, I. L., Jr., and Huneryager, S. G., *Human Relations in Management,* South-Western Publishing Company, 1960, 776 pp.

Heckman and Huneryager, *Management of the Personnel Function,* Merrill Books, Inc., 1962, 718 pp.

Hoslett, Schuyler Dean, *Human Factors in Management,* revised edition, Harper & Brothers, 1951, 327 pp.

Leavitt, Harold J., *Managerial Psychology,* University of Chicago Press, 1958, 335 pp.

Likert, Rensis, *New Patterns of Management*, McGraw-Hill, 1961, 279 pp.

Maier, Norman R. F.; Solem, Allen R.; and Maier, Ayesha A., *Supervisory and Executive Development*, Wiley & Sons, 1957, 330 pp.

McGregor, Douglas, *The Human Side of Enterprise*, McGraw-Hill, 1960.

Pigors, Paul; Myers, Charles A., and Malm, F. T., *Readings in Personnel Administration*, second edition, 1959, 554 pp.

Scott, William G., *Human Relations in Management*, Richard D. Irwin, Inc., 1962, 442 pp.

INDEX

A Accountability, in organization, 12
Agreement on method, in decision-making, 116, 117
Argyris, Chris, 25
Attention-gaining methods:
  devices, 71
  incongruity, 72
  timing, 72
Attitudes (see also **Morale**)
  explanation of, 27-29
  measurement, 29-34
"Audit," in communications, 31
Authority, in organization, 12
  overlapping, 14

B Bearing taking, in leadership, 100
Behavior patterns, in groups, 47
Bellows, Roger, 91
Belonging, in groups, 47
Benefits, from human relations training, 136, 137
"Buzz groups," in human relations training, 124

C Case studies, usefulness of, 136
Change, in decision-making, 111, 112, 118
Channels, in communications, 78-80
Chapple and Coon, 91
"Circle" chart, 8
Clarity, in communications, 73
Coca-Cola Company, 84
Committee organization, 9
Communications:
  attention gaining, 71, 72
  case study, 64
  channels, 78-80
  clarity, need for, 73
  counseling, 81, 82
  definition, 65
  factors in, 66-70
    motivation, 68-70
    semantics, 67
    sensory differences, 68
    verbalization, 66, 67
  "feedback," 65
  goals, 66

Communications (*Cont.*):
  informal, 80
  instructions, specific steps in, 73, 74
  "open door policy," 79, 80
  propaganda, 75, 76
  psychological barriers, 73
  public relations, 83, 84
  rapport, 76, 77
  rumor, 75
  source:
    formal, 74
    informal, 75
  timing, 72
  training:
    in listening, 70, 71
    in reading, 70, 71
  variety in approach, importance of, 69
Communications system, in morale measurement, use of, 31
Compensation, in Ego-defense, 57
Consultation group, in human relations training, 125
Consultative management, 10
Control, 12-14
  accountability, 12
  authority, 12
  responsibility, 12
  span, 13, 14
Cooperation and conflict in industry, 141
Counseling, 81, 82

D Decision-making:
  acceptance of decisions, 119, 120
  case study, 109-111, 118-120
  change, involvement of, 111, 112
  issues, determination of, 112, 113
  steps in, 113-118
    clarification of issue, 114-116
    evaluation of decisions, 117, 118